T0360608

Impact of COVID-19 on
Asian Economies and Policy Responses

Impact of COVID-19 on
Asian Economies and Policy Responses

Editors

Sumit Agarwal
National University of Singapore, Singapore

Zhiguo He
University of Chicago, USA

Bernard Yeung
National University of Singapore, Singapore

World Scientific

W JERSEY · LONDON · SINGAPORE · BEIJING · SHANGHAI · HONG KONG · TAIPEI · CHENNAI · TOKYO

Published by

World Scientific Publishing Co. Pte. Ltd.

5 Toh Tuck Link, Singapore 596224

USA office: 27 Warren Street, Suite 401-402, Hackensack, NJ 07601

UK office: 57 Shelton Street, Covent Garden, London WC2H 9HE

Library of Congress Cataloging-in-Publication Data
Names: Agarwal, Sumit, 1970– editor. | He, Zhiguo, 1977– editor. |
    Yeung, Bernard, 1953– editor.
Title: Impact of COVID-19 on Asian economies and policy responses /
    Sumit Agarwal, National University of Singapore, Singapore, Zhiguo He,
    University of Chicago, USA, Bernard Yeung, National University of Singapore, Singapore.
Description: Singapore ; Hackensack, NJ : World Scientific, [2020]
Identifiers: LCCN 2020038856 | ISBN 9789811229374 (hardcover) |
    ISBN 9789811229381 (ebook) | ISBN 9789811229398 (ebook other)
Subjects: LCSH: COVID-19 (Disease)--Economic aspects--Asia. |
    Asia--Economic conditions--21st century | Asia--Economic policy--21st century.
Classification: LCC HC412 .I429 2020 | DDC 330.95--dc23
LC record available at https://lccn.loc.gov/2020038856

British Library Cataloguing-in-Publication Data
A catalogue record for this book is available from the British Library.

Copyright © 2020 by World Scientific Publishing Co. Pte. Ltd.

All rights reserved. This book, or parts thereof, may not be reproduced in any form or by any means, electronic or mechanical, including photocopying, recording or any information storage and retrieval system now known or to be invented, without written permission from the publisher.

For photocopying of material in this volume, please pay a copying fee through the Copyright Clearance Center, Inc., 222 Rosewood Drive, Danvers, MA 01923, USA. In this case permission to photocopy is not required from the publisher.

For any available supplementary material, please visit
https://www.worldscientific.com/worldscibooks/10.1142/12072#t=suppl

Desk Editor: Tan Boon Hui

Typeset by Stallion Press
Email: enquiries@stallionpress.com

Printed in Singapore

Part I
Introduction

© 2020 World Scientific Publishing Company
https://doi.org/10.1142/9789811229381_fmatter

COVID-19: Collective Learning from the East

Sumit Agarwal,* Zhiguo He[†] and Bernard Yeung[‡,1]

*NUS Business School; Asian Bureau of Finance and
Economic Research
[†]Booth School of Business and Becker Friedman
Institute (China), University of Chicago; Asian Bureau of
Finance and Economic Research
[‡]NUS Business School; Asian Bureau of Finance and
Economic Research

A new virus was first reported in Wuhan towards the end of December 2019. China alerted the World Health Organization (WHO) of the unknown contagious virus on December 31, 2019. On January 7, 2020, China's officials announced that they had indeed identified a new virus,

---

[1] Sumit Agarwal is Low Tuck Kwong Distinguished Professor of Finance at the National University of Singapore Business School, Senior Fellow, ABFER, bizagarw@nus.edu.sg; Zhiguo He is Fuji Bank and Heller Professor of Finance, Booth School of Business and Director of Becker Friedman Institute in China, University of Chicago; and Senior Fellow, ABFER, Zhiguo.He@chicagobooth.edu; Bernard Yeung is Stephen Riady Distinguished Professor of Finance and Strategy, National University of Singapore Business School, and President of ABFER, byeung@nus.edu.sg.

2019-nCoV. Fast forwarding to the present, the highly infectious disease, now known as COVID-19, has spread globally and on March 12, 2020, WHO declared the situation a pandemic. By June 24, 2020, more than 9.4 million people around the world had contracted the virus and more than 481,000 were dead.

In order to mitigate the public health threat, a majority of countries implemented lockdowns to minimize face-to-face human interactions. However, many economic activities rely on such human-to-human interactions. Therefore, while these vigilant measures saved lives, they also generated a substantial negative supply and demand shock and significantly disrupted the global production value chain and trade. The consequence was a significant decline in output, a massive surge in unemployment, many bankruptcy cases, and worries over financial stability. On March 27, 2020, the Director of the International Monetary Fund (IMF) said that this economic setback is more severe than the Great Financial Crisis the world experienced in 2008–2009.

Asia's experiences with COVID-19 precede that in the West. Furthermore, many Asian countries had painfully experienced the Severe Acute Respiratory Syndrome (SARS) epidemic in 2003. Lessons drawn from Asia's experiences can benefit the world.

The community of the Asian Bureau of Finance and Economic Research (ABFER) has taken up the call to compile these insights to facilitate public information and understanding. Besides providing access to empirical and theoretical research on the pandemic conducted in the Asian context, these commentaries offer comprehensive information on the effects of the pandemic, the effectiveness of measures to contain the virus and the economic impacts of these measures. By deciphering the basic ingredients of government policies as well as their economic rescue packages, our commentaries shed light on the tradeoff between protecting public health and the economy. Finally, they address the impact of the pandemic on international trade, global value chains, and society. (These commentaries are written for ABFER circa in April 2020. While much has changed since, and some of the empirical observations may have evolved further, the insights are still very relevant.)

In the following paragraphs, we provide a summary of these commentaries in multiple segments.

I)   Containing COVID-19 and the Effects

The commentaries in this segment are mostly based on China's experiences. They provide a glimpse of the extent that China's lockdowns had dented industrial value-add and consumption. However, there is evidence that restricting inter-regional human mobility does mitigate the spread of the virus. Furthermore, the utilization of big data technology allowed China to separate the infected from the susceptible and thus reduce the spreading of the coronavirus without disrupting normal activities too extensively. One commentary notes that South Korea was successful in mitigating infection via effective tracking and quarantining without resorting to draconian lockdowns. Another points out that a government has the responsibility to contain a pandemic and provide remedial assistance; the long-term benefit being increased investment as exogenous risks are reduced. Finally, while a lockdown often sparked panic behavior on the goods market in the immediate term, Asian governments had taken constructive actions to contain the fallout.

1.   Qin Chen, Zhiguo He, Chang-Tai Hsieh and Zheng (Michael) Song
"Economic Effects of Lockdown in China"
This chapter reports that China's industrial value-add fell by 4.3% and 25.9% in January and February of 2020, respectively, on a year-on-year basis. The slump was dramatic, as prior expected growth is about 5.5%. The authors comment that "the economic impact of the lockdown on China is large, severe, [...] the recovery is sluggish in economic activities involving face-to-face interactions. The deteriorating pandemic situation across the globe is bringing an almost complete halt to the export sector in China and Chinese firms have difficulty accessing critical inputs provided by firms outside of China."

2.   Wenlan Qian
"A First Look at China's Consumption after Coronavirus"
The author highlights that from the outbreak of COVID-19 in late January to mid-April, 214 cities in China experienced an average of 32% decline in offline consumption. (These cities represent 90%

of China's urban population and account for 92% of China's GDP.) In aggregate, China lost over 1.2% of its GDP in 2019 through offline consumption in these twelve post-outbreak weeks. The drop was the worst in the most heavily infected city, Wuhan. There are a few noteworthy points. First, the daily consumption changes were negatively related to the day-to-day changes in the number of infections. Second, a renewed health threat slowed down recovery significantly. Offline consumption had almost fully rebounded as the infection rate receded by the end of March. Then, it fell again (16% below the baseline level) in mid-April when new infections surged. Third, while the decline in consumption is related to curtailed face-to-face human interactions and mobility, it is also due to looming uncertainty. Thus, to reinvigorate the economy, effective public health interventions to contain the spread of COVID-19 is critically essential.

3.   Hanming Fang
     "Public Policy Tools to Address the COVID-19 Pandemic: Health Versus Economy"
     The author describes the two crucial steps in dealing with the pandemic: (i) containing the spreading of the virus, e.g., testing, quarantining the infected, social distancing, and lockdowns, and (ii) expanding healthcare capacities. Asian countries have done a remarkable job in these areas. The author illustrates, based on his co-authored work, that the lockdown of the city of Wuhan (China), the epicenter of the coronavirus outbreak, reduced infection cases elsewhere in China by more than 50%. He also describes the success of South Korea in containing the spreading of the virus through reliable testing and targeted quarantining. South Korea's approach resulted in less severe economic disruption than lockdowns.

4.   Kairong Xiao
     "Saving Lives Versus Saving Livelihoods: Can Big Data Technology Solve the Pandemic Dilemma?"
     Lockdowns disrupt normal economic activities and, therefore, can be very costly. The author points out that big data technology may

help separate the infected from the susceptible without disrupting normal activities as much. The technology, however, infringes on privacy. The author describes China's experience to provide empirical light on the dilemma. On February 9, 2020, 17 days after the lockdown of Wuhan, Ant Financial (affiliated with Alibaba) developed the first health code application, which was first adopted by the Hangzhou municipal government. By the end of March, all Chinese cities had implemented the system. The app uses a smartphone's real-time location data to predict a holder's risks of being infected based on whether the holder is in close contact with confirmed patients. The app then uses the prediction to assigned a QR code to each smartphone holder — a green code allows free travel, yellow or red code means to be quarantined for 7 or 14 days, respectively. The codes turn back to green after the quarantine. Statistical results revealed that after the introduction of the health code app, the economic activities of a city adopting the app increased by around 2%–3% relative to other cities while human flow also increased. However, there was no corresponding increase in the infection rate. Overall, the use of big data technology created an economic value of 0.5%–0.75% GDP during the COVID-19 outbreak in China.

5. Harrison Hong, Neng Wang and Jinqiang Yang
   "Mitigating COVID-19 Risks to Sustain Growth"
   The authors argue that the policy to mitigate the economic damage of COVID-19 benefits an economy in the long run because providing social "insurance" against exogenous risks encourages investment. Their conclusion is based on their research on "climate change and sustainable growth." They build a model of a production economy. Then they simulate policy results allowing households' beliefs about the likelihood of exogenous disaster to vary. The simulation results show that there are long-term welfare benefits for costly mitigation. Their findings are consistent with what public health experts advocate (to act big and fast against COVID-19).

6. Yi Huang, Chen Lin, Pengfei Wang and Zhiwei Xu
   "Pandemic and Panic: Government as the Supplier of Last Resort"

This chapter argues that the pandemic and ensuing lockdowns sparked panic buying and hoarding of necessities, causing an acute shortage. The authors comment that China avoided such an outcome because the government limits purchases and is directly involved in the temporary production of essentials, e.g., surgical masks, which the private sector is unwilling to do. These measures help in curbing panic buying and hoarding. The authors use a bank-run model to illustrate that when left on its own, the private sector might have a self-sustaining sub-optimal panic equilibrium. Along the same line of thinking, the authors complimented China's government's building of mobile cabin hospitals in Wuhan in record time as well as pooling medical personnel from across the nation to the frontline in the fight against the virus.

II) Government Policies

The commentaries in this segment discuss government policy responses in dealing with the pandemic. After commenting on managing public health concerns, they raise a few noteworthy points. First, amidst the pandemic, at least before it starts to fade, containing the public health threat is more critical than reviving the economy. Empirical evidence shows that news on the former is associated with higher expectations on Gross Domestic Product (GDP) growth, while news on the latter is not. Second, while most governments deliver comprehensive and coordinated policies to people, businesses, and industries, country-specific factors drive differences in the desired government responses. For example, in China, providing companies financial support to mitigate massive layoffs is preferred to direct cash distribution to people. The reason is that Chinese households, holding significant precautionary savings, prefer job security.

Furthermore, Chinese state-owned corporations and banks have explicit responsibility in providing economic securities, and they are effective conduits to channel government aids to people. In the case of Singapore, residents traditionally expect the government to lead in coordinating and updating society-wide responses to the negative pandemic shock. In addition, there appears to be a certain sense of solidarity, built since the state's inception, to bring various social groups and corporations to share resources to counter the negative shock.

Third, empirical research shows that consistent and informative government communications and policies can avoid stirring up market volatility and negative sentiments. Asian governments have done amazingly well relative to their Western counterparts.

Finally, these Asia policies and practices may not be readily transplantable to other locations due to differences among regions in behavioral norms, cultures, and government priorities.

7. Hanming Fang

   "Six Lessons for Public Health in the Fight Against COVID-19"

   The commentary first advocates that containing a highly contagious disease calls for cross-country information and resource sharing, and the establishment of an International Health Fund. While mandatory lockdowns and social distancing can be effective in containing the spread of infection, additional means like testing is needed. While such approaches are costly and disrupt normal economic activities, putting an economy into a coma may be necessary for mitigating potent health threats. In the future, the stockpiling of vaccines and strategy medical supply would be required.

8. Keyang Li, Yu Qin, Jing Wu and Jubo Yan

   "Containing the Virus or Reviving the Economy? Survey from China Provides an Answer"

   The authors conducted a longitudinal online survey in February and March 2020 in multiple provinces in China. They show that, after controlling for individual fixed effects, a decline in the number of newly confirmed COVID-19 cases significantly increases its residents' expectations on GDP growth rate. They further find that the expectations are unaffected by reported real work resumption rate, estimated work resumption rate as produced by artificial intelligence, and even the respondents' own perceived work resumption rate. Their findings suggest that people's economic outlook only rises when the health threat abates.

9. Zhiguo He and Bibo Liu
    "Dealing With a Liquidity Crisis: Economic and Financial Policies in China During the Coronavirus Outbreak"
    Responding to the country-wide devastating adverse real and liquidity shocks, the Chinese government had undertaken several simultaneous approaches. First, via banks, it extended credit to frontline industries battling the epidemic and SMEs. Second, it expanded banks' ability to lend via relaxing bank reserve requirements and allowing local banks access to the central bank funds. Third, it raised larger corporations' ability to raise funds by lowering the restrictions in issuing corporate bonds for debt-repayment and allowing share pledged loans. Fourth, there is a set of policies to reduce firms' fiscal burdens, e.g., reduction and/or deferral on taxes, rents, fees, and mortgage payments. These policies closely match the business sector's "wishlist." While other countries are providing similar assistance policies, the authors point to some unique features in China: (i) China has high household savings and thus the help to households is tilted towards job preservation, (ii) the state-owned sector plays a more significant role than most countries in protecting employment, (iii) while participating in the financial assistance programs dents banks' profits, banks voluntarily play their part in these stabilizing programs.

10. Deborah Lucas
    "Policy Rx for the Economy: Cash or Credit"
    This chapter points out that the main objectives of government policies to combat the adverse economic effects of the coronavirus include: (i) address individuals' immediate hardships and cover basic needs; (ii) provide continuity and prevent permanent damage to individual livelihoods and organizational capital; and, (iii) bolster the resources available to the healthcare system. The author points out that, among the means to deliver, cash can be costly, while credit programs can be useful though not a silver bullet. The author raises useful principles in developing forbearance programs.

11. Joseph Cherian and Bernard Yeung
    "The State as Insurer of Last Resort"
    This commentary discusses Singapore's fiscal and financial policies in response to the pandemic. The policies illustrate well the generic elements of government policies to combat the adverse economic effects of the pandemic as highlighted in the previous chapter. For example, express cash delivery to low-income Singaporeans' bank accounts and to seniors' retirement savings accounts, financial forbearance programs to provide temporary relief to SMEs and to households having difficulties in meeting pre-committed payments and subsidies to mitigate job losses and preserve organization capital. The authors raise the point that there is an urgent need for political leaders to help citizens with lesser means.

12. Danny Quah
    "Singapore's Policy Response to COVID-19"
    This article analyzes Singapore's policies in countering the spread of COVID-19. On the public health front, the government has been keeping a watchful eye since December 2019 and has issued a steady and informative stream of public advisories since January 2020. It also offers free medical tests for viral infection and has prepared "stay-home" arrangements for the exposed with quarantine quarters for the infected. Technology has also been used to trace the origin and the transmission of the virus among people. On the economic front, the government has rolled out several budgets that aim to "stabilize and support" businesses and provide "care and social security" for individuals negatively affected by the pandemic. Frontline workers and industries also receive financial assistance. Finally, the government, led by the Prime Minister, has been maintaining consistent and accurate public release of information as well as effectively explaining comprehensive advisories on appropriate societal behavior. The Singapore government's clear and reassuring communication and leadership sharply contrast that in the US. In conclusion, the commentary reiterates the broad strands in Singapore government's policy response to the

COVID-19 outbreak: economic stability, scientific approach to build confidence, and political leadership in taking responsibility aided with clear and consistent communication.

13. Weina Zhang and Ruth Tan
"Singapore's Coordinated Battle Against the Pandemic"
This commentary continues the discussion of Singapore's government responses to the pandemic; it is useful because there has been further development after the previous chapter's commentary was written. An added angle in the commentary is the so-called "solidarity glue." Since the establishment of the state, the Singapore government emphasizes national unity and identity as well as family values. In managing the pandemic, the government, the corporate sector, and local communities cooperate earnestly to provide support for those hard-hit, e.g., foreign migrant workers. The pandemic has revealed many deep social conflicts and fault lines beyond a public health and economic crisis. Singapore may not be an exception. However, all sectors have managed to work together immediately to build remedies; this spirit is the foundation of Singapore's resilience and collective confidence.

14. Shang-Jin Wei
"Ten Keys in Beating Back COVID-19 and the Associated Economic Pandemic"
The author observes that while the spread of COVID-19 appears to have turned around in selected parts of Asia, the number infected is surging in the West. Western countries can ramp up their preparation by importing supplies from China, Japan and countries of relevant capacity, having a workable plan to ensure an adequate number of hospital beds especially intensive care unit (ICU) beds, adopting best practices in public communication, practicing social distancing and implementing its related policies, and offering assistance to businesses and workers to alleviate the negative impact of these public health control measures. The use of digital devices to curb the transmission is also advised. Additionally, an internationally coordinated economic stimulus program would be

more effective in reducing global recessionary pressure than isolated actions of individual countries. Also, cutting tariffs and nontariff barriers can help to fight a pandemic-inducted recession.

15. Xiao Ji, Mengyu Wang and Hong Zhang
   "Heuristics in Policymaking: It's Time to Figure Out What Drives Policy Uncertainty"
   In this commentary, the authors argue that policy responses may generate unintended consequences, e.g., confusion in policy responses may create market volatility and negative sentiments. Analyzing government announcements in Italy, Japan, Singapore, Taiwan, the UK, and the US, the authors demonstrate that policy uncertainty creates equity market volatility and dampens returns. Interestingly, Asian economies, exemplified by Taiwan, raise market volatility less and improve instead of damping market sentiment as reflected by immediate and near-term market returns.

16. Yueran Ma
   "What Comes to Mind: Some Reflections on COVID-19"
   In this commentary, the author reflects on belief formation, individual responses, and societal responses to the pandemic. First, she argues that people cannot imagine a far and remote happenstance from which they have no experience. This may explain why Westerners appear to be less sensitive to the infectious transmission of COVID-19 than Asians, who have previously experienced SARS. Second, the mitigation strategies to stop the viral contagion involves social distancing. However, this practice is to a large degree voluntary. It requires an individual sacrificing personal freedoms and face-to-face human interactions to reduce the risks of spreading the disease to strangers, on a "just-in-case" basis for she may or may not have been infected. Third, the government may not strictly enforce practices like social distancing and contact tracing. Adopting such mitigating policies depends on the government's priority, while their effectiveness depends on the valuation of individual freedoms and of traditional social behavior, like shaking hands and hugging.

III) Implications on International Credit and Trade

The pandemic has affected international credit and trade flow. Developing economies and emerging markets are expected to experience financial stress, especially if there are currency and term structure mismatch between their assets and liabilities. The asynchronous feature of the pandemic outbreak — first, Asian countries followed by Western economies — adds more uncertainty to the recovery of trade flows. Surprisingly, in the immediate period after the outbreak of the pandemic, disruption to the global supply chain is not steep while the subsequent negative demand shock may be. Still, in the longer run, the pandemic raises the value of resilience in the global value chains and further damages US–China relations. The world may move towards regionalism as a consequence.

17. Cyn-Young Park and Peter Rosenkranz

"The COVID-19 Pandemic Exposes Asian Banks' Vulnerability to US Dollar Funding"

The authors argue that the COVID-19 pandemic, together with the risk of a looming global recession, poses a significant threat to financial stability in Asia. Amid flights to safety and the unwinding of risky assets globally, the demand for, and the price of, the US dollar has soared. There is some evidence that in the past decade, banks in high-income Asian economies have increased their dollar lending while banks in emerging Asian economies have increased their borrowing denominated in the dollar. While Asia's banking system has improved its overall financial health, its exposure to global dollar funding markets and liquidity conditions has increased in tandem with its growing cross-border activities. In their plans to stabilize their economies and financial markets, Asian economies should remain vigilant to guard against a flare-up of financial vulnerability, given their high levels of debt and exposure to dollar funding risks. It is critical for national governments, regional organizations, and international financial institutions to work collectively to contain the economic fallouts of the pandemic and to support market confidence by strengthening the regional financial safety net. In the longer term, they need to contemplate how to deepen local currency bond markets further.

18. Bert Hofman
    "The Impact of COVID-19 on Asia and the Future of Global Supply Chains"
    The author first points out that East Asia has been most successful in containing the spread of COVID-19 and thus has experienced the least economic damage. The author shows that, according to the latest World Bank projection, East Asia and the Pacific is the only region to have positive growth in 2020. The region's much lower infection and death rates, compared to the West, are likely due to its people's strong inclination to wear masks, acceptance of social distancing, and its governments' strong lockdown measures. Interestingly, East Asian experiences suggest that the supply shock due to the pandemic could be manageable. From January to March 2020, when the pandemic was concentrated in East Asia, China's exports to and US's imports from ASEAN still registered positive growth. The concern is on the unfolding demand shock. Nevertheless, COVID-19 itself has intensified tensions between the US and China which will continue to disrupt international trade patterns and the global value chains.

19. Davin Chor
    "International Trade Has Suffered a One-Two Punch. Can It Recover After COVID-19?"
    The author cites that, stemming from the double whammy of the trade war and the pandemic disruption, US imports from China shrank 40% in February and March in 2020. These disruptions may have long-lasting repercussions. Firstly, the pandemic experience prompts firms to reassess their exposure to global supply value-chain disruptions; they will scale back offshoring. Secondly, in the name of keeping production of the essentials at home and preserving manufacturing capabilities, governments may intensify their protectionist rhetoric and measures. Thirdly, the pandemic

has tainted international cooperation, e.g., besides aggravating the US–China tensions, it has also raised tensions between the US and Canada and has weakened EU's solidarity.

20. Ben Charoenwong
    "COVID-19 in the Global Production Network"
    The author argues that the COVID-19 pandemic will dampen trade more significantly than SARS did in 2003 because global trade has expanded dramatically, particularly towards China. The importance of studying global production networks will likely increase as the world witnesses the wide-ranging effects of correlated supply disruptions. The author observes that the US–China trade war has prompted many firms to move their supply chains closer to their customers. It is unclear whether the pandemic will accelerate the movement because disruption due to a global exogenous shock is not diversifiable. However, firms will learn to seek more information on their supply chain risk exposures.

21. Hanming Fang and Bernard Yeung
    "Post–COVID-19 Reconfiguration of the Global Value Chains and China"
    This chapter's commentary discusses the configuration of the global supply chain and its aims to allocate production and serve customers efficiently. The economic calculus includes minimizing the sum of labor cost, transportation cost, and final assembly cost, as well as the cost to ascertaining resilience in the production value chain and customer access. Before the US–China trade war and the pandemic, containing production and transportation cost was paramount, which made China the world's manufacturing center. The intensified tension in US–China relations raises concerns about customer access and production resilience. Many in the business sector are now considering re-clustering resilient production around major consumption centers. The COVID-19 pandemic will simply expedite the reconfiguration. With a regional mindset in business planning, firms may make on-shoring investments in the US, China, and Southeast Asia. Firms will accept the efficiency-resilience tradeoff in supply chain regionalism while consumers

have to pay the price of the resultant inefficiency. The concern for China is that the consequent reduction in global competition may adversely affect China's inclination to develop its market and legal institutions further.

IV)   Concluding Remarks — A Post–COVID-19 World

22. Danny Quah
"Post–COVID-19, How Will We Be Better?"
This final chapter makes a few conjectures on what the post COVID-19 world may be like. For individuals, concepts like externalities, social responsibilities, individual privacy and freedoms, as well as authoritarian control have to be re-examined. In economics and businesses, COVID-19 accelerates the adoption of weightless arrangements using telecommuting technology. Very fundamentally, it makes us consider accepting redundancy in production systems: rebalancing the preference for global efficiency against the need for local resilience. Finally, the pandemic reveals many shortcomings in the state and market. Governments have to recognize that the efficiency of clustering (or super urbanization) has to be balanced against resilience stemming from spatial separation. They also have to step up their support for redundancy in medical equipment, vaccine discovery and production hitherto rejected by intensive market competition.

This is just the beginning. This is a marathon, not a sprint. COVID-19 will not disappear overnight and there is much more to think about and work on. Researchers across various disciplines are compiling long lists of questions for further study. The pandemic reveals that collective learning efforts and a humble attitude will benefit both the East and the West. We can make good use of a crisis!

We thank you for reading.

Sumit Agarwal, Zhiguo He and Bernard Yeung
August 2020

Contents

Part II

Containing COVID-19 and the Effects

© 2020 World Scientific Publishing Company
https://doi.org/10.1142/9789811229381_0001

Chapter 1

Economic Effects of Lockdown in China

Qin Chen,* Zhiguo He,[†] Chang-Tai Hsieh[†] and
Zheng (Michael) Song[‡]

*Business Big Data, Chengdu, China
[†]Booth School of Business, University of Chicago
[‡]Department of Economics, Chinese University of Hong Kong

On January 23, 2020, the Chinese government locked down the city of Wuhan (in Hubei Province). In subsequent days, similar measures were taken in other cities in Hubei and throughout China. This chapter documents several facts of the Chinese economy since the lockdown. The main findings are summarized below.

(1) The impacts of the lockdown on various economic activities, from flows of people and goods to aggregate output, were immediate and dramatic.
(2) Flows of people and goods out of Hubei have recovered to the pre-lockdown period. But daily visits to shopping malls and office buildings remain one third lower than the pre-lockdown level.
(3) The size and structure of consumption expenditure also experienced substantial adjustments.

3

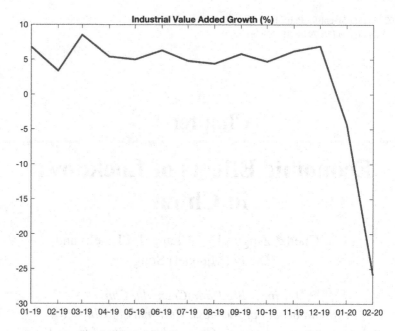

Figure 1.   Growth in industrial value-added (NBS).

All the changes are on a year-on-year basis.
Data source: WIND.

We begin with official data provided by China's National Bureau of Statistics (NBS). The most recent data (as of March 31, 2020) is from February 2020. Figure 1 shows that industrial value-added fell by 4.3% and 25.9% in January and February of 2020, on a year-on-year basis. If the counterfactual growth in absence of the epidemic is 5.7%, the average growth in 2019, the slump would be even more dramatic.

An alternative way to measure industrial output is data on shipment of goods across Chinese cities. We have data from a private trucking company that provides logistical services to truck drivers. This company, G7, has real-time GPS data from two million trucks, accounting for about 10% of all trucks operating in China. We aggregated the movement of trucks in and out of a provincial capital by day. Figure 2 plots the daily truck flows between provincial capital cities, with the beginning day of the year normalized to one. The decline of truck flows before the Wuhan lockdown

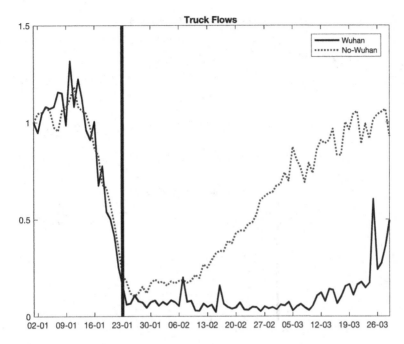

Figure 2.   Truck flows among provincial capital cities.

The black bar marks the start of the Wuhan lockdown. The solid and dotted lines are for truck flows that involve and do not involve Wuhan, respectively. We use the 2018 regional trade flow data as weights for aggregation.

Data source: G7.

captures the slowdown associated with the coming Chinese New Year. Strikingly, the truck data suggests goods flows between Wuhan and the other provincial capital cities remained at a very low level and did not recover until mid-March.

Figure 2 also shows that truck flows among the other provincial capital cities recovered to the pre-lockdown level at the end of March. The halt of goods flows in late January and early February is consistent with the dramatic decline (−26% as shown in Figure 1) of industrial output in February.

The next set of data we show are flows of people within and between cities. Here, we use indices of movements of people provided by Baidu. This data is based on location-based services in Baidu Map. Figure 3 plots

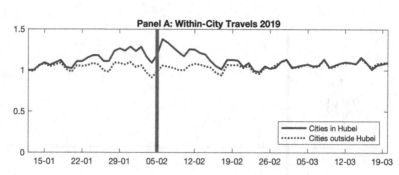

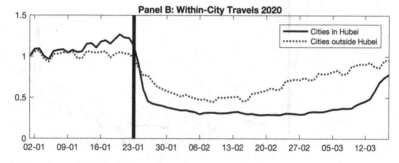

Figure 3.   Baidu within-city travel index.

This figure plots within-city travel intensity with the beginning day of the year normalized to one. Panels A and B plot the data for 2019 and 2020, respectively. The bar in Panel A marks the 2019 Chinese New Year. The bar in Panel B marks the start of the Wuhan lockdown, two days before the 2020 Chinese New Year. The solid and dotted lines are for within-city travels in and outside Hubei, respectively. We use city population in the 2010 census as weights to aggregate city-level indices.

travel intensity within a city, with the beginning day of the year normalized to one. Panel A and Panel B plot the data for 2019 and 2020, respectively. The bar in Panel A marks the 2019 Chinese New Year. The bar in Panel B marks the start of the Wuhan lockdown, which was two days before the 2020 Chinese New Year and exactly precedes the free fall of travels within a city in Hubei. The index dropped by more than half within a three-day window and remained low for six weeks, only to pick up recently until mid-March. The indices outside Hubei were picking up more rapidly and had almost reached the level in early January.

The movement of people across Chinese cities were more severely affected, as shown in Figure 4. The travels to/from cities in Hubei were

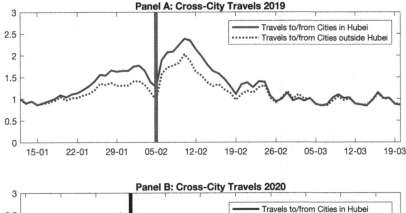

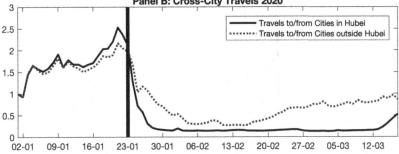

Figure 4.   Baidu cross-city travel index.

This figure plots cross-city travel intensity, with the beginning day of the year normalized to one. Panels A and B plot the data for 2019 and 2020, respectively. The bar in Panel A marks the 2019 Chinese New Year. The bar in Panel B marks the start of the Wuhan lockdown, two days before the 2020 Chinese New Year. The solid and dotted lines are for cross-city travels that involve and do not involve cities in Hubei, respectively. Baidu provides data on travels to and from each city. The cross-city travel index is the average of inflows to and outflows from a city. We use city population in the 2010 census as weights to aggregate city-level indices.

nearly frozen. The cross-city travels that do not involve Hubei cities also experienced sharp declines, though to a lesser extent than those involving Hubei cities. In mid-March, the cross-city travels outside Hubei had fully recovered to the early January level.

While flows of goods and people outside Wuhan have more or less recovered, the impacts of lockdown appear to be persistent on economic activities involving personal interactions. We obtain location data provided by the three major mobile carriers in China. We use this data to measure the number of people in shopping malls and office locations in Chinese cities.

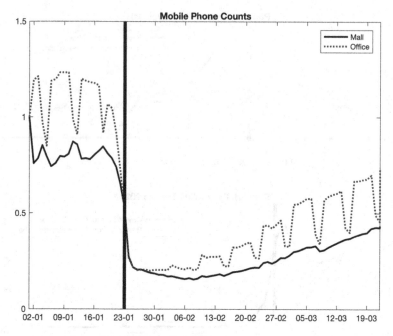

Figure 5.   Visits to office buildings and shopping malls.

This figure plots cross the average of visits to shopping malls (solid line) and office buildings (dotted line) across Chinese cities in the past three months, after normalizing the number of people in a location to 1 on January 2, 2020. Again, the vertical line denotes the date of the start of lockdown in Wuhan.

We geocoded the location of the main shopping malls. Based on these geocodes, we measured the number of people in each of these locations in a given day. Figure 5 shows the average of this number across Chinese cities in the past three months, after normalizing the number of people in a location to 1 on January 2, 2020. Again, the vertical line denotes the date of the start of lockdown in Wuhan. Before the lockdown, the figure shows clearly the cycles of work and shopping within a week, as the number of people in offices (shopping malls) falls (rises) over the weekend. We see a sharp decline of both population flows after the Wuhan lockdown. The number of people in office buildings seems to recover quicker; however, the recovery is far from complete despite the steady increase after mid-February. The number of visits to shopping malls and office buildings were about half of their pre-lockdown levels by the fourth week of March.

Adjustments to consumption were also swift and sizable. The official data shows that total retail sales of consumption goods dropped by 21% in January and February from a year earlier. The food service income fell by 43%, which is consistent with the equally dramatic decline of visits to shopping malls in Figure 5.

To gain more understanding of the consumption response to the lockdown, we further obtained monthly sales data by product category from a major online platform in China. Panel A of Figure 6 shows a dramatic shrink of digital and electronic goods sales in January and February 2020, which used to account for two thirds of total sales from the platform before the lockdown. The adjustment was striking in Hubei, where more than two thirds of digital and electronic goods sales evaporated in January

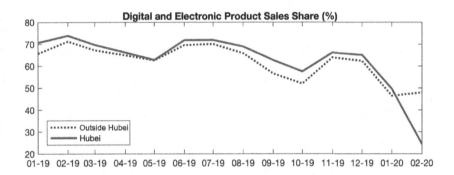

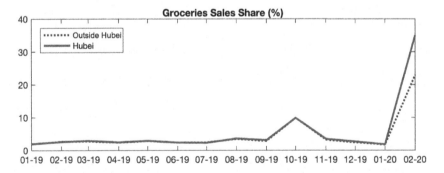

Figure 6. Online sales shares by product category.

This figure plots monthly digital and electronic goods sales share (Panel A) and groceries sales share (Panel B) on a year-on-year basis. The solid and dotted lines represent sales in and outside of Hubei, respectively. The data is provided by a major online sales platform in China.

and February. Panel B shows the flip side of the shift. Groceries now account for more than 35% and 23% of total sales in and outside of Hubei, respectively.

In sum, the economic impact of lockdown on China is large, severe, and perhaps is still mounting. While flows of people and goods outside Hubei have come back to their pre-lockdown levels, the recovery was sluggish in the economic activities involving face-to-face interactions. The top authorities in Beijing are rolling out various massive economic and financial policies in a timely fashion. Nevertheless, at this point, China is still facing a daunting challenge to economic recovery. The deteriorating pandemic situation across the globe is bringing an almost complete halt to the export sector in China, and could make it difficult for Chinese firms to access critical inputs provided by firms outside of China.

© 2020 World Scientific Publishing Company
https://doi.org/10.1142/9789811229381_0002

Chapter 2

A First Look at China's Consumption After Coronavirus

Wenlan Qian

NUS Business School, National University of Singapore;
Asian Bureau of Finance and Economic Research

With countries engaging in distancing and mobility-restriction measures to contain the spread of COVID-19, a central policy debate lies in the tradeoff between stringent public health interventions and the severe economic ramifications that come with those interventions.

However, a lack of an effective public health response carries negative implication for the economy as well. Knowledge is inconclusive concerning the transmission mode, rate of spread, and lethality, and no effective medical cure of the novel coronavirus exists, making projection of the course of the pandemic difficult. The huge uncertainty directly hurts consumers' willingness to consume when they feel unsafe and anxious, even with no imminent threat of economic security. Figuring out the appropriate balance requires a good understanding of the magnitude as well as the nature of the problem due to the unprecedented nature of the event in the past century.

In a recent working paper,[1] we provide direct evidence on the consumption impact of COVID-19, drawing upon China's experience from the start of the outbreak to mid-April 2020. Early facts about the economic impact of COVID-19 in China are valuable as other countries are starting to go through a similar experience with COVID-19. China was the first country to experience a large-scale outbreak in January 2020, giving us a sufficiently long post-outbreak period to identify the pattern. The Chinese government implemented draconian measures, including locking down Wuhan, as well as strict measures to distance the population and to close non-essential service businesses in other cities. Many other infected countries or regions subsequently followed suit with similar measures.

We use daily offline consumption data aggregated at the city level as recorded by UnionPay's card and QR scanner spending transactions (i.e., including spending using both bank cards and e-wallets linked to Alipay or WeChat pay). UnionPay is China's largest offline payment provider with a 30% market share of the country's offline consumption (source: China UMS and National Bureau of Statistics). The 214 cities in our sample cover 92% of China's 2018 GDP and 90% of the country's urban population. To isolate the effect of COVID-19, we conduct difference-in-differences analysis by using the daily offline consumption data during the same period in 2019 as the control period.

Our key findings are two-fold. First, the consumption consequences are grave after Wuhan's lockdown. Looking at the raw consumption data (Figure 1), offline consumption for the 214 cities in the sample declined dramatically in 2020 relative to 2019. The average difference in total offline consumption of the 214 cities between the post-Wuhan-lockdown period and the pre-Wuhan-lockdown period in 2020 is 8.06 billion RMB. Difference-in-differences estimate suggest that daily offline consumption dropped by 32% on average across the 214 cities, or 18.57 million RMB per city, during a 12-week period relative to the change in the benchmark period (2019).

---

[1] Haiqiang Chen, Wenlan Qian and Qiang Wen. 2020. "The Impact of the COVID-19 Pandemic on Consumption: Learning from High Frequency Transaction Data." Working Paper. https://papers.ssrn.com/sol3/papers.cfm?abstract_id=3568574.

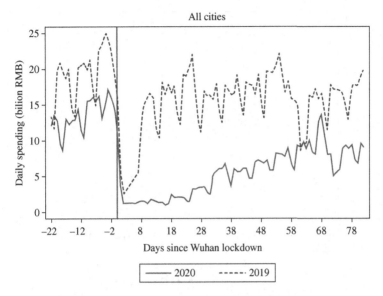

Figure 1. Offline consumption comparison.

We observe a prevalent consumption decrease across the 214 cities in our sample. Heavily exposed cities, such as Wuhan, saw their offline consumption reduced by 70% during the 12-week period. As Figure 2 indicates, the cross-city variation in the total number of COVID-19 cases explaining 23% of the variation in the average consumption decline in the 8-week period.

Second, city consumption responded negatively to the day-to-day changes in epidemic severity in the same city. For example, doubling the infected cases in a city was followed by a 4.9% greater decrease in the same-city's consumption. When the public health situation worsened, consumption plummeted, and vice versa.

Consistently, we observe signs of offline consumption recovery, which appears to trace the epidemic situation (see Figure 3). The consumption change became less negative starting from the fifth week. By the end of March, consumption had fully rebounded. However, consumption fell again, ending at 16% below the baseline level in mid-April. This retreat is responsive to the one-day lagged number of new infections (including asymptomatic cases), echoing the rising concern over a potential second wave of infections.

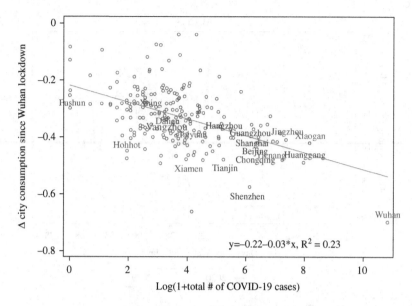

Figure 2.   Consumption decline after Wuhan lockdown.

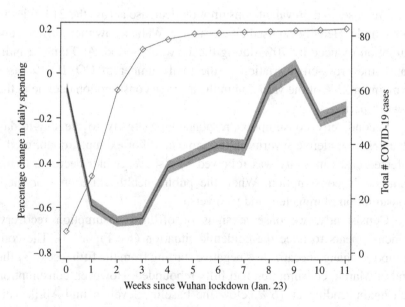

Figure 3.   Offline consumption recovery.

These results are informative in the following ways. The large decline in offline consumption is closely related to the strict public health measures, which significantly restricted people's physical activities and affected business and job security. The findings thus highlight the importance of prompt and adequate policy interventions to alleviate the negative impact especially on the more affected sectors such as retail and certain service industries. Our finding implies China lost over 1.2% of its GDP in 2019 through offline consumption in the 12-week post-outbreak period, providing an informative ballpark estimate of the effect magnitude, as many countries start to go through the same experience.

Furthermore, we believe the consumption decline was also driven by a reduced consumer demand arising from the large uncertainty regarding the length and trajectory of the epidemic exposure. Within each city, we see a strong and negative consumption sensitivity to daily measures of the outbreak severity, including the number of confirmed cases, stress on the hospital capacity, and occurrence of the first COVID-19 death. Such a relationship is not explained by the mobility-restriction measures or macroeconomic conditions that varied at a much lower frequency in the period. This suggests an ignored value of an effective public health intervention in reinvigorating our economy. The pandemic induces large uncertainty and discourages consumer demand, and massive economic relief programs may still result in a limited effect without an effective public health intervention to contain the spread of COVID-19.

© 2020 World Scientific Publishing Company
https://doi.org/10.1142/9789811229381_0003

Chapter 3

Public Policy Tools to Address the COVID-19 Pandemic: Health Versus Economy

Hanming Fang[1]

*University of Pennsylvania; Asian Bureau of Finance and
Economic Research*

The COVID-19 pandemic is impacting our lives in unprecedented ways. The Novel Coronavirus is very contagious with an R0 value estimated to be 2.5. That is, in the initial stage of the epidemic, every infected person will infect 2.5 people on average. Moreover, people can be infectious yet asymptomatic. There are several public policy strategies to deal with the growing pandemic.

1. First are strategies aiming to delay the spread of the virus, including quarantining infected persons and their contacts, lockdowns and restrictions of human mobility, and social distancing such as prohibiting public gatherings and limiting public transportations. The goal of these policies is to **flatten the infection curve**, and manage the

---

[1]Prof. Hanming Fang is Class of 1965 Term Professor of Economics, University of Pennsylvania and Senior Fellow, ABFER.

growth of infected patients so as not to overrun the healthcare system.

2. Second are strategies to expand the capacities of the healthcare system, including purchasing new equipment, building temporary hospitals, recruiting retired healthcare workers and volunteers, and moving idle capacity in less impacted to more severely impacted areas.

Lockdowns and other mobility restrictions are effective in delaying and containing the spread of the coronavirus. My co-researchers and I find in our empirical research that in China, the lockdown of the city of Wuhan, which is the epicenter of the coronavirus outbreak, from January 23, 2020, reduced infection cases elsewhere in China by more than 50%.

However, lockdown measures came with severe negative impacts on the economy. Recent data shows that the Chinese industrial value-added declined by about 25% in February 2020 relative to the same month last year. The lockdown measures implemented in the US has already led to a record number of unemployment claims. Economic indicators point toward a pandemic-induced recession; some have even predicted a depression.

Any good policy needs to balance the tradeoff between health and economy. What are the alternatives? It is useful to take a look at the approach taken by South Korea, which is extensive testing plus **targeted** quarantines. Instead of a wholesale lockdown, only individuals confirmed with the virus and their contacts are quarantined. These result in smaller impact on the economy. There are two necessary conditions for the Korean approach: (1) Tests are quick, accurate, and readily available; (2) Extensive social contact tracing is feasible. The US is definitely making progress in the first condition. But the social contact tracing may be more limited in the US because of the Health Insurance Portability and Accountability Act of 1996 (HIPAA) protection of private health information.

Before scientists develop a proven vaccine and an effective therapeutic treatment, we are, unfortunately, faced with this tough tradeoff: protecting the population's health, and avoiding a deep recession, which itself can cause many harms to overall population health and public safety.

© 2020 World Scientific Publishing Company
https://doi.org/10.1142/9789811229381_0004

Chapter 4

Saving Lives Versus Saving Livelihoods: Can Big Data Technology Solve the Pandemic Dilemma?

Kairong Xiao

Columbia University

Pandemics such as COVID-19 present an difficult choice to policymakers between saving lives and saving livelihoods. On the one hand, economic lockdown is deemed necessary to contain the rapid spread of the disease. On the other hand, a lockdown inflicts steep economic costs as normal activities are disrupted. The painful tradeoff between human toll and economic costs has led to heated and sometimes divisive debate in the policy domain.

How can we solve the pandemic dilemma between saving lives and saving the economy? Many believe that the answer lies in big data technology. Using huge volumes of data produced by smartphones, we may detect potential carriers of the disease and break the transmission chains. At the same time, big data technology can also identify groups of people who are unlikely to carry the disease so that they can resume normal work and life, which limits the economic damage of the disease. Advocates often cite the successful experiences in China and South Korea where big data technology was aggressively deployed to combat the virus.[1]

However, big data technology is also highly controversial. Critics argue that some countries such as Singapore have seen little success from using contact-tracing apps.[2] Implementing big data technology could also divert critical resources from proven containment methods such as aggressive testing. Big data technology may also disproportionately impact the rights of those under- or misrepresented by the data.[3] Finally, big data technology also raises concerns about privacy infringement and government surveillance. Therefore, using big data to address the public health crisis can potentially do more harm than good.

This chapter sheds light on this debate by studying the effectiveness of big data technology in mitigating the economic and human costs of the COVID-19 outbreak in China. I exploit the staggered implementation of a contact-tracing app called "health code" in 322 Chinese cities amid the COVID-19 pandemic. On February 9, 2020, 17 days after the lockdown of Wuhan, the first "health code" was developed by Ant Financial, a FinTech company afflicted with Alibaba, and adopted by the Hangzhou municipal government, where Ant Financial's headquarters is located. This app uses real-time location data produced by smartphones to predict holders' risks of being infected, based on whether the holders have been in close contact with confirmed patients. This app assigns a QR code for each holder, which functions as a "traffic permit" within the city. As shown in Figure 1, there are three color codes. Holders of a green code can travel freely around in the city; holders of yellow or red codes have to be quarantined for 7 or 14 days, respectively. The codes turn back to green after the quarantine. Health code was subsequently expanded to other cities in China. By the end of March 31, all cities in China had implemented

---

[1] See Forbes April 9, 2020 article "The Vital Role of Big Data in The Fight Against Coronavirus".

[2] See WSJ April 22, 2020 article, "Singapore Built a Coronavirus App, but It Hasn't Worked So Far".

[3] For instance, the April 12, 2020, AP News article "Europe eyes smartphone location data to stem virus spread" reports that Israeli government's cell phone location-tracking program has caused complaints that the authorities are erroneously confining people to their homes based on inaccurate location data.

杭州健康码

【绿码】

凭码通行

【黄码】

实施7天内隔离，连续
（不超过）7天健康打卡正常
转为绿码

【红码】

实施14天隔离，连续14天
健康打卡正常转为绿码

防 控 疫 情　　人 人 有 责

Figure 1.   Hangzhou health code. From left to right: green code, yellow code and red code.

this system. The staggered adoption of health code represents the largest experiment of big data technology in the public health domain. It offers an invaluable opportunity to examine the effectiveness of big data technology in mitigating economic and human costs inflicted by pandemics.

To measure high-frequency variations in economic activities at the city level, I used within-city population movements constructed from smartphone locations by Baidu and daily emission of greenhouse gases related to industrial activities. Figure 2 plots the national average within-city movement in the sample period. To control for the effect of the Lunar New Year, I normalized the level of within-city movement using the same day value of the 2019 lunar calendar. I reported the value as a percentage of the average value in the first week of 2020. Figure 2 shows a steep drop in economic activities after January 23, 2020, the day that Wuhan began its lockdown. The second vertical line indicates February 9, 2020, the date that the Hangzhou health code was introduced. The graph shows that within-city movement slowly recovers in mid-February. By the end of the

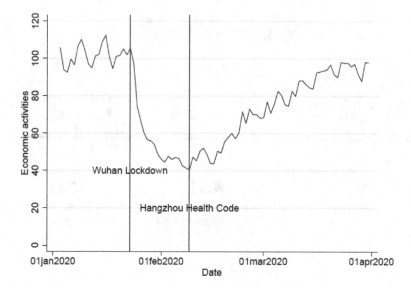

Figure 2.   Economic activities of chinese cities.

sample period, the within-city movement has rebounded to about 95% of the pre-COVID-19 level. I further examine the emission of greenhouse gases such as nitrogen dioxide and obtain similar patterns of economic recovery.

The empirical analysis yields two main results. First, I find that the introduction of the health code app significantly increases economic activities as measured by within-city population movements and greenhouse gas emission. The dynamic treatment effect of the health code can be visualized in Figure 3. Before the introduction of the health code app, there is no pre-trend between the treated and control cities, suggesting that the parallel trend assumption seems to hold in the data. After the introduction of the health code app, the economic activities of the treatment cities increase by around 2%–3% compared to the controlled cities. Furthermore, I find that cities that implemented the health code app attract greater population inflows and experience smaller population outflows.

Second, I find that the introduction of the health code app has significantly reduced the infection growth rate of COVID-19. Figure 4 reports the dynamic effect of the introduction of the health code app on infection

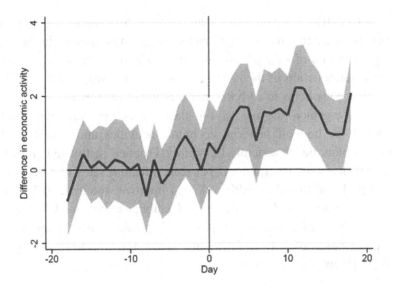

Figure 3. Difference in economic activities in treated and control cities.

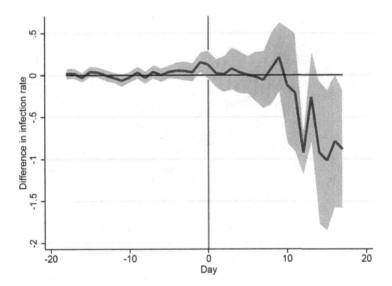

Figure 4. Difference in infection rates in treated and control cities.

rates of COVID-19. Again, there is no pre-trend between treated and control cities suggesting the parallel trend assumption is satisfied in the data. The growth rate of newly confirmed cases significantly drops ten days after the introduction of the health code app, which suggests that the big data technology helps to curb the transmission of the virus.

Taken together, the use of big data technology has significantly improved the tradeoff between economic activities and public health. Figure 5 plots the "Pandemic-Possibility Frontier" estimated from the data, which shows the trade-off between infection rates and economic activities. I find that the health code app improves the tradeoff between economic activities and virus infection. I calibrate an SIR model using the estimates. The model shows that the use of big data technology created an economic value of 2% of GDP and saved 190,000 lives during the COVID-19 outbreak in China.

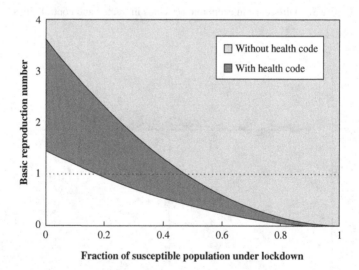

Figure 5.   Trade-off between economic activites and COVID-19 infection rate.

© 2020 World Scientific Publishing Company
https://doi.org/10.1142/9789811229381_0005

Chapter 5

Mitigating COVID-19 Risks to Sustain Growth

Harrison Hong,* Neng Wang[†] and Jinqiang Yang[‡]

*Columbia University; National Bureau of Economic Research;
Asian Bureau of Finance and Economic Research
[†]Columbia University, National Bureau of Economic Research;
Asian Bureau of Finance and Economic Research
[‡]School of Finance, Shanghai University of Finance and Economics

Synopsis

The debate about the economic fallout from the arrival of COVID-19 is increasingly framed as an either/or — sacrificing the economy through mitigation strategies such as social distancing or imperiling millions of lives. We argue that this framing misses the benefits of mitigation for the economy in the long run. Even holding fixed important moral considerations, the planner's solution to a model of a production economy where households face economic disaster risks point to significant benefits of spending real resources on mitigation. If households' belief regarding pandemic arrival rates weighs a really bad scenario, such as uncertain vaccine effectiveness and recurrent COVID-19 waves that negatively impact productivity and capital stock, then the optimal solution calls for drastically ramping up mitigation spending to curtail such disaster risk. Mitigation crowds out consumption, investment, and lowers the value of capital in the short run. But it ensures sustainable economic growth and delivers higher social welfare in the long run.

Introduction

The economic fallout from the arrival of the COVID-19 pandemic and mitigation attempts through social distancing have been abrupt. Stock markets have fallen as much as 35% (as of March 24, 2020) and there are forecasts of prolonged consumption and investment slowdowns. The debate on the optimal level of mitigation is increasingly framed as a trade-off of protecting lives at the expense of the economy. Whether from tweets by President Trump or newspaper opinion editorials, the phrase "flattening the curve" has come to symbolize this unfortunate tradeoff. So compelling has been this framing that Lt. Governor Dan Patrick of Texas, 69, said on the Tucker Carlson show on March 24, 2020 "Those of us who are 70 plus, we'll take care of ourselves. But don't sacrifice the country."

We argue that this either/or framing does not account for potentially important benefits of mitigation to the economy. Even holding fixed important moral considerations, we show that there are also long-term welfare benefits or pure growth arguments for costly mitigation or suppression strategies.

Our thesis — that mitigation curtails COVID-19 risks to insure sustainable growth — is elaborated on below.[1] We present the planner's solution to a model of a production economy where households learn from exogenous disaster arrivals about whether arrival rates are frequent or rare but can spend resources to mitigate permanent disaster damages to tangible physical or intangible (be it human or organizational) capital, conditioned on arrival. The optimal planner solution maximizes growth and welfare for households in the long run. The aggregate risk of the economy is endogenously driven by decisions regarding mitigation and investments

---

[1] Our thesis is adapted from Hong, Wang, and Yang (2020b). It is related to Hong, Wang, and Yang (2020a), who show that corporate valuations would be significantly lower absent mitigation for COVID-19.

due to household intertemporal preferences over consumption and implied demand for risks.

While our model can be applied to a wide range of disasters such as climate change,[2] we think it is particularly apt for COVID-19. As Bill Gates' 2015 prescient TED Talk on pandemics points out, mitigation is ideally spending on preparedness like an efficient testing system (as South Korea has been doing). Social distancing — as many countries have been forced to do in the absence of efficient testing systems — is a far more costly form of mitigation. We do not model choices of mitigation strategies. Rather we assume that in the absence of mitigation spending, the arrival of a pandemic will have significant negative effects on output; but as mitigation spending rises, the negative impact falls.

Rationale for Mitigation

The solution to our model in Figure 1 emphasizes the optimal response depending on households' belief about arrival rates of disasters. Details of our calibration, which follow work of Barro and Jin (2011) and Pindyck and Wang (2013), can be found below. The parameter values including risk aversion and time preference of households, productivity, and the return and volatility to capital, are set to capture realistic scenarios.

We assume that households consider two scenarios of pandemic arrivals: the good scenario is a low arrival rate of roughly once every 25 years and the bad scenario is an arrival rate of around once every two and a half years. The bad scenario corresponds to recurrent pandemic waves which occurred during the 1918 Flu or in the longer run a higher arrival rate of other viruses. As agents do not know the true underlying state, they learn over time from realized disasters.

We plot the responses of mitigation spending (panel A), consumption (panel B), investment (panel C) and value of capital (Tobin's average q) (panel D) to beliefs regarding a bad scenario with high arrival rates (i.e. the x-axis), where a belief of π at zero means households believe the

---

[2] For instance, Hong, Wang, and Yang (2020b) quantify the value of seawalls to reduce the risks of more frequent Atlantic hurricane arrivals due to global warming.

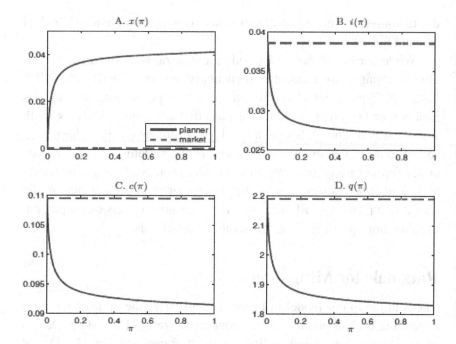

Figure 1. This figure plots mitigation-spending-to-capital ratio $x(\pi)$ (panel A), investment-to-capital ratio $i(\pi)$ (panel B), consumption-to-capital ratio $c(\pi)$ (panel C), and the value of capital $q(\pi)$ (panel D) as functions of π, belief regarding pandemic arrival rates. $\pi = 0$ is the most optimistic belief in a low arrival rate and $\pi = 1$ is the most pessimistic belief in a high arrival rate.

economy is in the good scenario while a belief of π at one means households believe the economy is in the bad scenario.

There are two lines — a solid line that describes the scenario when households have access to mitigation technology and a dashed line that corresponds to the scenario where households do not have access to mitigation. For instance, societies in the 1918 Flu did not believe in social distancing as an effective mitigation tool and hence it was much less used than today (Hatchett, Mecher and Lipsitch, 2007). When households believe in the good state, the two lines touch.[3]

---

[3] We have chosen the mitigation technology parameter so that the planner's solution optimally chooses no mitigation even with access to the technology in the most optimistic scenario, i.e., $\pi = 0$.

We are interested in understanding what the optimal mitigation response is even if households put just a little bit of weight on the bad scenario. The optimal mitigation spending is highly non-linear and increasing very sharply with belief about the bad scenario. We ramp up mitigation from no spending to spending around 2% of the capital stock when the belief π is around 5% (panel A). In contrast, even when the household believes entirely in the bad scenario ($\pi = 1$), the mitigation spending is a little over 4%.

Connecting this plot to COVID-19, we started with placing little weight on the bad scenario (i.e. our π was close to zero). The arrival of COVID-19 has now increased (or at least should increase) our belief in the bad scenario. This optimal non-linear ramping up effect provides a justification for a rationale for utility-maximizing households to engage in suppression strategies (i.e., extreme mitigation). The point of mitigation is not simply dealing with the current fallout but also insuring against future fallouts. That is, our belief in the bad scenario might drift up in the future; hence part of the economic fallout today also captures mitigation spending meant to address additional pandemic risks down the road, including predicted follow on waves from COVID-19.

Mitigating now and aggressively comes at the expense of investment, consumption, and the value of capital (panels B–D). Notice in panels B–D the dashed lines corresponding to the no-mitigation scenario are flat even as beliefs worsen. We have intentionally picked preference parameter values (specifically, we set a key parameter, the elasticity of intertemporal substitution, to one, an empirically reasonable choice) so that the investment-capital ratio, the consumption-capital ratio, and capital valuation multiple (e.g., Tobin's average q) all remain constant (without mitigation) even as beliefs deteriorate. Doing so allows us to single out the impact of mitigation by analyzing the solid lines.[4]

Insuring Economic Growth

Why is the optimal solution so non-linear and sharply increasing initially in beliefs about arrival rates? This can be seen in Panel A of Figure 2,

---

[4] The main results on the effects of mitigation continue to hold provided that we choose an elasticity of intertemporal substitution that is larger than one. This is a key condition that is required to match asset-pricing moments as first pointed out by Bansal and Yaron (2004).

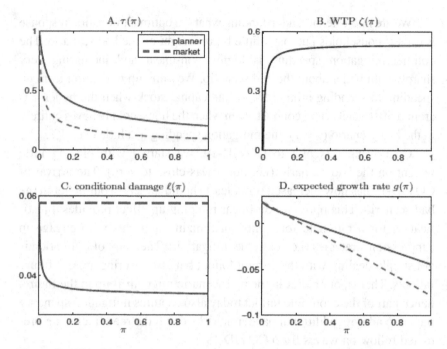

Figure 2.   This figure plots the welfare and growth implications of optimal mitigation strategy. Panel A reports a welfare measure proportional to certainty equivalent wealth. Panel B reports the gain of the household's certainty equivalent wealth due to mitigation as a fraction of her certainty equivalent wealth in the absence of mitigation. Panels C and D report the expected loss $l(\pi)$ and the expected growth $g(\pi)$, respectively.

where we plot household welfare measured by the certainty-equivalent wealth.[5] Without mitigation, we see the certainty-equivalent wealth declines dramatically and non-linearly with beliefs (the dashed line). In contrast, the certainty-equivalent wealth (the solid line) drops much less and stays above the dashed line because mitigation generates substantial downside protection (curtailment or loosely hedging benefits) which leads to higher social welfare.

In Panel B, we plot the welfare cost of not using the available mitigation technology (the ratio between the solid and the dashed line in Panel

---

[5]To be precise, the variable on the y-axis in Panel A is the certainty-equivalent wealth given belief is scaled by the certainty-equivalent wealth when the household believes the economy is in the good state for sure. That is why both curves start at one when $\pi = 0$.

A). The welfare cost is substantial even when the probability attached to the bad scenario is low. For example, even with $\pi = 5\%$, households demand an 80% increase of the capital stock from the current level as compensation for not using the available mitigation technology.

In Panel C, we show that optimally using the mitigation technology lowers the expected losses due to disasters. Moreover, the more pessimistic the household, the greater the benefit of curtailing disaster risk (as we see from the widening gap between the two lines).

In contrast, the effect of mitigation on the expected growth rates (including the effect of disasters) is subtler. For low levels of beliefs, the household is sacrificing some expected growth as immediate cuts to consumption and investment are substantial and the immediate effect of curtailing risks on growth are not yet very high (due to the low odds of disasters arrivals). Therefore, the expected growth rate with optimal mitigation strategy could be lower than with no mitigation.

However, as households become more pessimistic (i.e., more weight on the bad scenario), they are better prepared with mitigation than without for future disaster arrivals. As a result, optimal usage of mitigation significantly buffers growth slowdown by reducing the expected damages upon the arrival of disasters. This plot captures the essence of mitigation to insure sustainable economic growth.

Other Implications for COVID-19 Pandemic

What about the gloomy economic forecasts post–COVID-19? As our model predicts, some of the economic contraction is for the purpose of a more sustainable growth path going forward. Of course, our model does not capture financial frictions, moral hazard, and other important behavioral consideration in the economy. These factors, which played an important role in the Great Recession of 2008, are undoubtedly appearing again. But Federal Reserve Bank and Treasury policies should be able to address some of these excesses in the short and medium terms. Moreover, Hong et al. (2020) documents how damage to corporate earnings depend on a high vaccine arrival rate.

Nonetheless, none of this changes our basic policy conclusion which is consistent with those of public health officials in "acting fast and acting big" against COVID-19, though our argument is entirely based on sustainable growth reasons. Our thesis is also in agreement with a recent editorial in the *Washington Post* by Lawrence Summers in which he argues that discussions of mitigation miss the point that the arrival of COVID-19 means that mitigation strategies go hand in hand with long-run economic welfare (Summers, 2020).

The forces we have pointed out here also apply to longer term risks we face with climate change. The last few years has seen increased interest in sustainability issues from across large segments of the economy as beliefs regarding climate change have shifted (Hong, Karolyi and Scheinkman, 2020). While COVID-19 will no doubt dominate our focus in the near term, it is also a wake-up call to step up our research on the adjustment of the economy to climate disasters predicted by scientists that are coming down the road.

References

Bansal, R. and Yaron, A., 2004. Risks for the long run: A potential resolution of asset pricing puzzles. *The Journal of Finance,* 59: 1481–1509.

Barro, R.J. and Jin, T., 2011. On the size distribution of macroeconomic disasters. *Econometrica,* 79(5): 1567–1589.

Gates, W., 2015. The next outbreak? We are not ready. *TED Talk.*

Hatchett, R.J., Mecher, C.E. and Lipsitch, M., 2007. Public health interventions and epidemic intensity during the 1918 influenza pandemic. *Proceedings of the National Academy of Sciences,* 104(18): 7582–7587.

Hong, H., Karolyi, A. and Scheinkman. J., 2020. Climate Finance. *Review of Financial Studies,* 33: 1011–1023.

Hong, H., Kubik, J., Wang, N., Xu, X. and Yang, J., 2020. Pandemics, vaccines and corporate earnings (No. w27829). *National Bureau of Economic Research.*

Hong, H., Wang, N. and Yang, J., 2020a. Implications of Stochastic Transmission Rates for Managing Pandemic Risks. *Review of Financial Studies,* forthcoming.

Hong, H., Wang, N. and Yang, J., 2020b. *Mitigating Disaster Risks in the Age of Climate Change,* SSRN Working Paper.

Pindyck, R.S. and Wang, N., 2013. The economic and policy consequences of catastrophes. *American Economic Journal: Economic Policy,* 5(4): 306–339.

Summers, L., 2020. Trump is missing the big picture on the economy. *Washington Post,* March 25.

© 2020 World Scientific Publishing Company
https://doi.org/10.1142/9789811229381_0006

Chapter 6

Pandemic and Panic: Government as the Supplier of Last Resort[1]

Yi Huang,* Chen Lin,[†] Pengfei Wang[‡] and Zhiwei Xu[§]

*Graduate Institute, Centre for Economic Policy Research
[†]Faculty of Business and Economics, University of Hong Kong
[‡]Peking University HSBC Business School; Hong Kong
University of Science and Technology
[§]Shanghai Jiao Tong University

Introduction

The COVID-19 pandemic has caused a global health and economic crisis. As of May 4, 2020, the number of confirmed cases has surpassed 3.5 million, with more than 248,000 deaths around the world so far. The pandemic also sparked panic buying and hoarding of critical medical products by members of the public, as well as a significant surge in unnecessary hospital visits. How governments deal with these issues is critical to their overall response to the pandemic and their ability to end the crisis.

---

[1]Acknowledgments: We would like to thank Bengt Holmström, Wenlan Qian, Yijiang Wang, Yi Wen, Liyan Yang and Bernard Yeung for thoughtful discussions and suggestions. We also thank Melody Guo for research assistance.

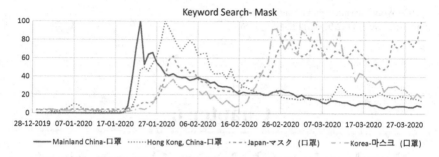

Figure 1.   Internet searches for masks (Google trends and Baidu).

When the coronavirus outbreak started in China, concerned citizens started panic buying medical products such as masks almost immediately. The immediate and dramatic increase in demand can be illustrated by the number of searches for masks on the Google and Baidu search engines (Figure 1). As can be seen from the Google and Baidu data, when COVID-19 started to spread in mainland China and Hong Kong, searches for masks reached their peak in 10 days. This was faster than the rate of actual infections, indicating panic buying was already underway. Hospitals were also quickly flooded by patients worried that they had contracted the virus, which severely strained their resources and meant that many patients with serious conditions unrelated to the virus could not be promptly treated.

Economists in China engaged in a heated debate about whether and how the government should regulate the prices of affected medical products. The price of non-medical masks in China increased from a base index value of 100 on January 19, 2020 to an index value of 656 on February 19, 2020, representing a 556% increase over a month. The price of surgical masks and N95 masks also increased by between 200% and 340% compared to the previous month (Figure 2). If we look at the price of meltblown fabric, the core material of medical masks, this also shows a ten-fold increase in a month, from US$5,673 per ton in early February 2020 to US$56,737 a ton on February 28, 2020 (Figure 3).

There were generally two perspectives. Pro-market advocates argued that the panic buying reflected a significant and actual discrepancy between supply and demand, and the government should therefore not

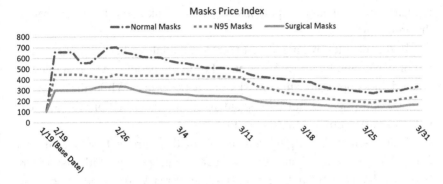

Figure 2. Mask price index in China.

Source: Shenzhen Government Procurement Center, http://cgzx.sz.gov.cn/ztlm/qlzhyqfkctzfcglstd/fywzjgzs/202004/t20200407_19153848.htm.

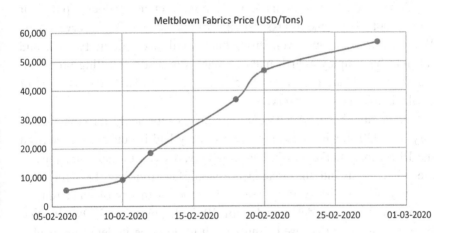

Figure 3. Market price of meltblown fabric.

Source: New Retail Business Review, https://xw.qianzhan.com/analyst/detail/329/200304-72788f3f.html.

interfere by imposing price regulations. The surge in market prices was a strong signal for manufacturers to increase production. Others argued, though, that supply and demand was too simple a lens to apply to price dynamics during periods of turmoil when people are not being rational actors. The invisible hand, they said, had failed to help the market achieve efficient allocation. However, both arguments are based upon canonical demand-supply theory — perhaps we could think about the issue from a different angle.

In this chapter, we argue that there is an analogy between panic buying of masks and historical bank runs. For many people, the pandemic has created the impression that masks are a necessity. While the surge in demand and prices is indeed a spontaneous market reaction, the demand is largely driven by precautionary motives.

In this sense, the surging demand for medical products such as masks is much the same as a bank run.[2] As such, we propose to study the underlying mechanisms behind the panic buying of masks from the perspective of a classic bank run. Understanding the principle behind this phenomenon could be helpful for governments to address the root cause of the problem.

A bank run occurs when a large number of clients suddenly pull their money out of a bank. Banks usually do not keep 100% reserve funds. When faced with runs, even strong banks will face a liquidity crisis and fall into bankruptcy, which makes a bank run a self-fulfilling prophecy. During a mask shortage, a mask retailer acts like a bank and its stock of masks is like the bank reserve.

Bank runs have caused economic crises repeatedly throughout history. In 1930, for instance, the US economy had begun to recover from the 1929 stock market crash. Unfortunately, a series of bank runs pushed the US economy into the Great Depression. Bank runs have been recorded as early as the 17th century, although a formal theory of bank runs in economics was not developed until 1983. Diamond and Dybvig, two American economists, used simple math to describe in detail the bank's function of liquidity creation. The logic behind the theory is very intuitive. In general, investors demand long-term funds to finance their projects while savers demand short-term liquidity to meet their current needs, with banks pooling the funds of both parties to solve the liquidity mismatch problem. In normal times, banks hold a certain amount of reserves and the remaining funds are provided to investors in the form of long-term loans.

---

[2] See Wang and Xu (2020) for more recent discussions about the mask run in China during the outbreak of coronavirus, link: https://www.yicai.com/news/100485707.html.

However, Diamond and Dybvig proved there is disequilibrium during a bank run. The mechanism works as follows. The bank intrinsically cannot recall long-term loans to meet short-term demand for liquidity because it does not maintain sufficient reserves. Once depositors become concerned about the risk of a bank run, they rush to withdraw their money before others to ensure the safety of their funds. This panicked behavior creates negative consequences and shared pain for individuals, leading to market failure.

Back to the panic buying of masks caused by the coronavirus pandemic. Like bank runs, the panic prompted many people to purchase and hoard masks before they sold out, which we will refer to as a "panic run." Due to limited daily production capacity, this behavior placed people with an urgent need for masks, such as medical workers, at even higher risk. This in turn slowed containment efforts, which again increased the frenzied public demand for masks. Even worse, sellers began to anticipate that prices would surge further and started hoarding masks in anticipation of greater profits, exacerbating the shortage. This spiral caused the market to fail to allocate masks efficiently. In the following section, we provide a simple model to regulate panic run behavior.

A Simple Panic Run Model

We consider a two-period simple model, $t = 1, 2$. The economy has one unit measure of population. There are two types of people: the low infection risk group (type L) with measure $\alpha \in (0, 1)$ and the high infection risk group (type H) with measure $1 - \alpha$. We assume there is a medical product that can protect people from infection. In the model, we use masks as a specific example. The main analysis also applies to other protective products or medical services relating to the coronavirus.

In period 1, the producer can supply $y_1 \leq m < 1$ units of masks at a marginal cost of $\phi > 0$. In period 2, the producer can supply $m - y_1$ units of masks at a marginal cost of $\phi > 0$. We assume that the type H agents will be infected with the virus in the absence of the protection of a mask. However, in period 1 there is zero risk of the type L agents being infected.

We assume that the momentum disutility of infection is $-V$, hence the utility gain derived from wearing a mask is V for type H agents, and zero for type L agents. We assume that the type L agents will become the high-risk type in period 2 with probability $\theta \in (0, 1)$ due to the spread of the virus, and wearing a mask can prevent them from being infected. So the expected utility of wearing a mask for type L agents is θV. We assume that V is sufficiently large such that

$$\theta V > \phi. \tag{1}$$

In period 2, the number of infected agents is $1 - \alpha + \alpha\theta$. We further assume that the total stock of masks m satisfies

$$1 - \alpha + \alpha\theta < m < 1. \tag{2}$$

The last condition implies the stock of masks can cover all of the agents with high exposure risks in the first two periods, but it cannot meet the demand if every agent buys masks in period 1. We assume in the latter scenario that masks are sold on a first-come first-serve basis. In the case of medical services, m may correspond to the number of frontline health-care workers.

A panic run under exogenous price

We first consider a case of exogenous price where the price of a mask in two periods is equal to the marginal cost, i.e. $P_1 = P_2 = \phi$. As in the Diamond–Dibvig bank run model, there exist two equilibria: the normal equilibrium, where no agent engages in surge buying of masks; and the panic run equilibrium, where the panic buying of masks occurs in period 1.

Normal equilibrium

Only type H (high-risk) agents buy masks in period 1, and type L (low-risk) agents just wait and buy masks in the second period if they become the high-risk type. During the equilibrium, the net utilities (compared to the situation without the protection of masks) for both types of agents satisfy

$$U_H = 2V - \phi \quad \text{and} \quad U_L = (V - \phi)\theta. \tag{3}$$

The total demand for masks is then given by $1 - \alpha + \alpha\theta$, which is lower than the total supply m. Therefore, a run does not occur. Notice that each agent's decision is optimal in the sense that no one has the incentive to deviate. Given others' strategies, individual type L agents obtain a net utility of $-\phi + V\theta$ if this deviates, which is lower than U_L. For each type H agent, it is obvious that the deviation drives a net utility of zero, which is lower than U_H.

Panic run equilibrium

In this equilibrium, if both types of agents rush to buy masks in period 1, then the total demand is 1. However, each of them can get the masks only with a probability of $\frac{1}{m}$ due to the limited supply. Therefore, the expected net utilities for both types of agents are given by

$$\widehat{U}_H = (-\phi + 2V)\frac{1}{m} \quad \text{and} \quad \widehat{U}_L = (\theta V - \phi)\frac{1}{m}. \tag{4}$$

Again, in this panic run equilibrium, no one has the incentive to deviate since they will obtain a zero net utility if they deviate and wait until the next period. Therefore, these two equilibria are self-fulfilling.

Pricing mechanism

One natural question is whether the market mechanism, i.e. raising the price, can solve the problem of the shortage caused by the run. To answer this question, we further endogenize the price of masks. We will show that it is more likely to cause opposition. The market pricing mechanism may actully worsen the severity of the mask shortages.

We assume that in period 1 the price is fixed at marginal cost, i.e. $P_1 = \phi$, and the market condition endogenously determines the price in period 2. For the supply side, we now allow the sellers to decide how many masks to sell in period 1. If the sellers believe $P_2 > P_1 = \phi$, they may have a strong incentive to hoard the masks in period 1 and sell them afterward.

Let s denote the fraction of high-risk agents who fail to buy the masks in the first period. We assume that the probability of type L agents becoming type H, θ, is increasing in s, i.e. $\theta'(s) > 0$. This assumption characterizes the positive externality of wearing the masks during the pandemic. In the second period, $\theta(s)\alpha + (1 - \alpha)s$ fraction of the total population is at high risk of exposure and demand the protection of masks. Thus, the total demand for masks in period 2 is $\theta(s)\alpha + (1 - \alpha)s$. A lower fraction of type H agents obtaining masks in period 1 (s is high) induces a higher demand for masks in period 2. We further assume that the stock of masks m satisfies

$$\theta(0)\alpha + 1 - \alpha < m < \theta(1)\alpha + 1 - \alpha. \tag{5}$$

The above condition implies that the maximum production of masks can cover the demand in a normal situation where every type H agent can obtain masks in period 1 (i.e. $s = 0$), but it cannot meet the demand under a panic situation where no type H agents get masks (i.e. $s = 1$). Besides, analogous to the case of exogenous price, we assume $\theta(0)V > \phi$. Again, there exist two equilibria.

Normal equilibrium

In this equilibrium, no panic run occurs. The prices in two periods are equal to the marginal cost, $P_1 = P_2 = \phi$. The sellers behave competitively and receive zero profit. The net utilities for both types of agents are $U_H = -\phi + 2V$ and $U_L = (V - \phi)\theta(0)$, respectively. Analogous to the previous analysis, in this equilibrium each agent has no incentive to deviate, given others' strategies. Sellers also have no incentive to deviate. This is because the total demand in period 1 and period 2 is $\theta(0)\alpha + 1 - \alpha$, which is less than the total supply of masks m, implying a buy-side market. Therefore, the price P_2 must equate to the marginal cost ϕ. The zero-profit condition deters the sellers' hoarding behaviors for masks in period 1, which confirms the equilibrium conditions on the demand side.

Panic run and hoarding

In this disequilibrium, similar to the case of exogenous price, the panic run occurs. However, the situation becomes even worse when the market conditions endogenously determine the price. Since we assume that the price is fixed in period 1 ($P_1 = \phi$), the sellers now have a strong incentive to hoard all of the masks and wait until the second period to sell them. This hoarding behavior is optimal for the sellers since, in period 2, they can sell at a higher price. To see this, remember that if the sellers hoard the masks, no agent, including the high-risk group, can get masks in period 1, i.e. $s = 1$. Therefore, in period 2 the total demand for masks is $\theta(1)\alpha + 1 - \alpha$, which exceeds the total supply m (see Eq. [5]). The market for masks is now on the seller's side, where the price is set to the marginal value of the buyer, $P_2 = V$. This equilibrium is the worst scenario with the lowest level of social welfare, as none of the high-risk agents can obtain the masks in the first period, and more people are exposed to the virus.

Policy Implications and China's Experiences

The question now becomes: How can we alleviate the panic buying of scarce medical resources during a pandemic? The bank run theory can inspire a potential solution. After the invention of the Diamond–Dybvig model, economists wrote thousands of papers on how to end bank runs. Two measures are mentioned most often. The first is to stop cash withdrawals to prevent a bank run from the demand side. The other is to establish a deposit insurance system (DIS) to consolidate the safety of deposits from the supply side. The DIS requires a central bank that can provide unlimited liquidity to support it.

Two similar measures could help solve the problem of panic runs. The first is to directly curb demand. In the case of a mask shortage, this could be achieved by imposing tighter restrictions on the buying of masks in those areas less severely affected by a virus, or creating a lottery to limit mask purchases. For example, if the government mandated that exactly $1 - \alpha$ unit of masks should be sold in the first period, this would eliminate the panic run equilibrium in the first price equilibrium. Knowing there will be $m - (1 - \alpha) > \alpha\theta$ masks left in the second period, type L agents would have no incentive to buy masks in the first place. However, this is feasible only if the government knows the truth fraction of both types. As discussed above, if the seller can increase their price in the second period, government restrictions on purchases in the first period would not be useful.

In the early stage of the coronavirus outbreak in China, some of the above measures were implemented by local governments. Similarly, in the case of medical services, the policy could be to require infected patients with mild symptoms to self-isolate. However, it should be noted that although the above measure could curb panic buying, it does not substantially enhance allocation efficiency or optimize social welfare. Even worse, there would be a potential risk of increasing transmission of the virus.

The second potential measure is for the government to establish its own production base. For medical products such as masks, it is not profitable for other enterprises to switch to mask production for a short period due to slow regulatory approval processes and the fact that the surge in demand is temporary. Thus, the market has limited ability to expand the supply in the short term. Therefore, as a last resort, the government should quickly begin its own production while still guaranteeing product quality. These production facilities should be part of the national public health system, which plays a similar role as the deposit insurance system as a supplier of public goods. After all, during a pandemic, a critical medical product such as a mask becomes a public good because it creates a positive externality by curbing the spread of the virus.

When the coronavirus outbreak began in Wuhan, the whole city experienced an acute shortage of medical products and services such as N95 surgical masks and hospital beds. The Chinese government then issued a series of virus-containment edicts that generally followed the logic of the second type of measures discussed above. The central government also created a stimulus package, including fiscal and monetary instruments for the expansion of production capacity for anti-virus-related goods and services. According to official statistics, the production capacity of masks in China increased from 20 million per day to 116 million per day within a month. This rapid expansion in the supply largely mitigated the public panic over masks. To solve the acute shortage of hospital beds amid the outbreak, China also started building temporary hospitals almost immediately. When Wuhan went into lockdown, two temporary hospitals, the Huoshenshan and Leishenshan facilities, with a combined total of 2,600 beds, were completed and started to operate within two weeks. Also, the Wuhan municipal government built 14 temporary medical stations to treat patients with mild symptoms. Many other cities also built similar hospitals as a precautionary measure. Other provinces around China sent more than 40,000 doctors and nurses to Hubei province to support frontline healthcare. These measures largely mitigated public panic over the availability of medical services, and effectively stemmed the spread of the virus in that country.

To prepare for the next pandemic, governments should create strategic inventories of essential medical supplies and equipment. They should also increase their systemic capacity to treat patients. At the same time, as this research suggests, they can take effective measures to reduce panic runs, which will allow scarce medical resources to be allocated to those who need them most.

References

1. Diamond, D.W. and Dybvig, P.H., 1983. Bank runs, deposit insurance, and liquidity. *Journal of Political Economy*, *91*(3), pp. 401–419.
2. Huang, Yi, Lin, Chen, Wang, Pengfei and Xu, Zhiwei, 2020. Saving China from the coronavirus and economic meltdown: Experiences and lessons, 2020, in VOXEU e-book *Mitigating the COVID Economic Crisis: Act Fast and Do Whatever It Takes*, link: https://voxeu.org/article/saving-china-coronavirus-and-economic-meltdown-experiences-and-lessons.
3. Wang, Pengfei and Xu, Zhiwei, 2020. Mask Panic as Bank Run, *Yicai*, link: https://www.yicai.com/news/100485707.html.

Part III

Government Policies

© 2020 World Scientific Publishing Company
https://doi.org/10.1142/9789811229381_0007

Chapter 7

Six Lessons for Public Health in the Fight Against COVID-19

Hanming Fang

University of Pennsylvania; Asian Bureau of Finance and Economic Research

We are probably too early to discuss all the lessons we can learn from the fight against COVID-19. But let us start with the following six early ones.

Lesson 1: *Infectious viruses know no national boundaries, thus international coordination and cooperation are essential.*

In our tightly connected global economy, no country can stand on the sideline and just watch other countries fight the virus. This means that countries need to share information and resources. Just like we need to move idle healthcare capacity from one state to another domestically to fight the spread of the virus, such mutual assistance should occur among nations as well. A much better funded and staffed **International Health Fund**, akin to the International Monetary Fund, to coordinate global responses to public health crises should be on the agenda as humanity deals with the threats from pandemics.

47

Lesson 2: *Mandatory lockdowns and social distancing are effective in slowing down the spread of the virus infections.*

Infection diseases grow exponentially at the initial stage of an outbreak. If unchecked, the rapid growth of infected patients is likely to overrun most of the healthcare system. Strategies aimed to delay the spread of the virus — including quarantining infected persons and their contacts, lockdowns and restrictions of human mobility, and social distancing such as by prohibiting public gatherings and limiting public transportations — have proven to be effective to "flatten the infection curve", which can help spread out the burden on the healthcare system.

Lesson 3: *Testing is key to slow down the spread of the virus, especially when people who contracted the virus can be asymptomatic yet infectious.*

Communities and countries that conducted mass testing or extensive testing of anyone who might have been exposed to the virus, seem to have done well in containing the spread of the virus. A small northern Italian town of *Vo Enganeo* was home to Italy's first death from COVID-19 on February 21; it was put on a lockdown and tested all 3,300 residents. This mass testing revealed that about 3% of residents were infected with the virus, and of these, about half did not show any symptoms. The town isolated all of the infected and has not reported any new cases since March 13. South Korea also did extensive testing and was able to flatten its infection curve very effectively. In order for the US economy to safely reopen, we must have quick, accurate, and readily available tests for the virus and antibody against the virus.

Lesson 4: *Mandatory lockdowns are economically costly. Deep economic recession has its own negative health consequences. The tradeoff between health and economy is real and needs to be discussed front and center.*

So far, the public face of the fight against COVID-19 is the public health experts, and rightly so. However, as a nation progresses in the infection curve, economic consideration must be brought to the front and center. Mandatory lockdown measures come with severe negative impacts on the economy. Recent data shows that the Chinese industrial value-added declined by about 25% in February 2020 relative to the same month last year. The lockdown measures implemented in the US has already led to record number of unemployment claims. Within three weeks of the COVID-19 pandemic hitting the US, 17 million unemployment claims were filed as of the week of April 4, 2020. Economic indicators point toward a pandemic-induced recession; some even predicted a depression that may be deeper than the Great Depression. Social isolation during the lockdown and the economic depression from prolonged lockdown have their own serious negative health consequences.

This tradeoff makes it all the more important to have readily available, quick, and accurate tests so that segments of the economy or regions can be reopened, while protecting vulnerable populations and continue to engage in cautious voluntary social distancing.

Lesson 5: *COVID-19 shock to the economy is unlike any other shocks in recent history. We need to put the economy in a "coma" temporarily so as not to damage the vital organs of the economy, allowing it to spring back to life once the shock passes.*

It is a demand shock, as large segments of the economy are shutdown, such as airlines, tourism, and most of the service sector. But the right public policy response is not to stimulate demand. It is a supply shock as workers are locked down at home, but supply-side stimulus is not the right policy response either because we need the outbreak to pass before getting workers back to their jobs. The economic policy to address this shock needs to put the economy into a "coma," keeping all the vital organs of the economy intact so that it can spring back to life once the shock passes. It is a new challenge. On the positive side, this shock is exogenous, and policymakers do not have to worry about moral hazard in rewarding "bad behavior." This differs from the Great Recession of 2007–2009.

Lesson 6: *Support scientific research; and stockpile the strategic medical supply reserves.*

The value of science cannot be clearer in this pandemic, as vaccines and therapeutic cures are ultimately what will end the spread of the virus. Stockpiling of strategic medical supply reserves are also clearly imperative.

© 2020 World Scientific Publishing Company
https://doi.org/10.1142/9789811229381_0008

Chapter 8

Containing the Virus or Reviving the Economy? Survey from China Provides an Answer

Keyang Li,* Yu Qin,[†] Jing Wu[‡] and Jubo Yan[§]

*Hang Lung Center for Real Estate, Tsinghua University
[†]Department of Real Estate, National University of Singapore
[‡]Hang Lung Center for Real Estate, Tsinghua University
[§]School of Social Sciences, Nanyang Technological University

During the COVID-19 public health crisis, policymakers face a tough tradeoff between containing the coronavirus using aggressive measures such as lockdown and stay home quarantine, and reviving the economy which encourages the continuation of normal economic activities. Our research team conducted an online survey tracing the same individuals over a few weeks from late February to mid-March this year, aiming to understand whether individuals' expectations on economic prospects are more affected by the severity of the COVID-19 epidemic, or the level of ongoing economic activities. In other words, do people care more about containing the disease or sustaining normal economic activities when forming their economic expectations during an epidemic?

We designed and implemented an internet-based survey (in Chinese) of three waves (February 29 to March 2 for wave 1, March 6 to 8 for wave 2, March 12 to 14 for wave 3) tracking approximately 1,900 of the same individuals from seven provinces in China (Hubei, Hunan, Sichuan, Guangdong, Liaoning, Inner Mongolia and Fujian). Our respondents were sampled from a wide range of age groups with a good mixture of different education backgrounds and income levels. In each wave, we asked the respondents their prediction on some economic indicators in the first quarter of 2020, including the year-on-year (y-o-y) real GDP growth rates of Q1 2020 of the nation, Hubei province, and their own provinces. It is worth noting that we offered additional cash rewards (60 yuan, approximately S$12) to the respondents if their prediction was very close to (within ± 0.2 percentage point) the actual economic growth rate in Q1 2020 to be released in mid-April by the National Bureau of Statistics in China, so that they would have an incentive to answer the questions seriously.

Figure 1 shows our respondents' prediction on the GDP growth rate in Q1 2020 in China. In addition, we also sought respondents' perception on the GDP growth rate in 2019 to capture their level of familiarity with GDP

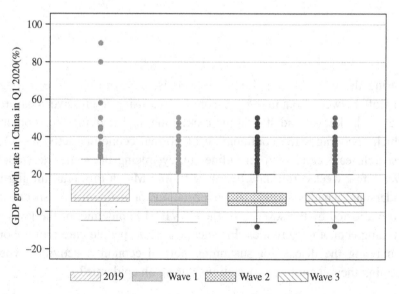

Figure 1.   Prediction on GDP growth rate in Q1 2020.

growth rate. The results showed that the COVID-19 epidemic negatively affects the individual's expectation on economic growth. The median respondent believed that the GDP growth rate in China in 2019 was 7% (the actual GDP growth rate in China was 6.1% last year). However, the median respondent believed that the GDP growth rate in China in Q1 2020 would be 5.3%–5.5%, which is 1.5–1.7 percentage points lower than their perceived growth rate last year.

Given the negative effect of COVID-19 on individual's expectation on economic prospects, a natural question is, how can such negative impacts be mitigated? In particular, which target should be prioritized, containing the virus or sustaining normal economic activities?

To answer this question, we first link individuals' revision on their GDP growth predictions between the two waves with the number of newly confirmed COVID-19 cases in their city between the two waves in a regression analysis. Our result suggests that lower number of new COVID-19 cases in a city between the two waves significantly increases local residents' expectations on GDP growth rate. **On average, a one standard deviation (107) reduction of new COVID-19 cases within the past 6–7 days would lead to an upward revision of GDP in China in Q1 2020 by 0.289%. In particular, a switch from positive number of new cases to zero causes an upward revision of GDP growth rate in Q1 2020 in China by 0.718%.** Overall, the results suggest that, in an epidemic such as COVID-19, the success in containing the virus will lead to a significant upward revision of economic growth expectation among individuals.

Next, we aim to understand whether higher level of economic recovery during the COVID-19 epidemic can also mitigate the negative impact of COVID-19 on economic expectations. In wave 2 and wave 3 of the survey, we ask the respondents their perceived work resumption rate in China on the survey date. On average, the perceived work resumption rate was 42.6% in wave 2 (6–8 March) and 47% in wave 3 (12–14 March). We incorporate their perceived work resumption rate in the regression model and find that their perceived change of work resumption rate is not correlated with their update on GDP growth rate predictions. Nonetheless, individual's perception of work resumption rate is likely to be affected by the severity of COVID-19 in their local city, or correlated with their personal characteristics, such as education background and social economic status.

To more rigorously test whether work resumption rate would affect individual's prediction of GDP growth rate, in wave 3, we randomly divided the respondents into five groups. We first asked the respondents to predict GDP growth rate just like the previous two waves, then provided them with a page of information on work resumption rate in China.

In the baseline group (T0), we provided the current average level of work resumption rate in China measured by the AI experts at Tsinghua University, which was 65.6% on March 11, 2020. In the other four treatment groups, we provided additional information on the work resumption rate in some selected cities, including the major city with the highest (T1) and lowest (T2) levels of work resumption rates, Beijing (T3), and the provincial capital of the individual's residing province (T4). The allocation of groups was based on random numbers generated from our survey software. After reading the information, we gave the respondents the chance to revise their predicted GDP growth rate, if they wished to.

Our analysis suggests that individuals do not update their belief on economic expectations when randomized information on work resumption rate is provided. Specifically, individuals neither revise their expectation based on the perception gap of the work resumption rate, nor respond to different ways that the information is presented. **The results indicate that the level of economic recovery, regardless of how the information would be presented, have little or no impact on individuals' economic expectations.**

These findings jointly suggest that, during an epidemic such as the COVID-19, containing the virus can substantially mitigate the negative impact of an epidemic on individuals' expectations on economic prospects, while sustaining normal economic activities may not be effective in maintaining positive economic expectations among individuals.

Although our study focuses exclusively on mainland China, the findings can convey valuable policy implications to other major economies which are now fighting the COVID-19 pandemic. In the tradeoff between containing the coronavirus using aggressive lockdown or quarantine measures and encouraging the sustaining of normal economic activities, **containing the spread of virus should be prioritized over continuing economic activities, at least from the perspective of maintaining positive economic expectation among individuals.**

© 2020 World Scientific Publishing Company
https://doi.org/10.1142/9789811229381_0009

Chapter 9

Dealing With a Liquidity Crisis: Economic and Financial Policies in China During the Coronavirus Outbreak

Zhiguo He* and Bibo Liu[†,1]

*Booth School of Business, University of Chicago; Asian Bureau
of Finance and Economic Research
[†]PBC School of Finance, Tsinghua University

The coronavirus outbreak that began last December sharply curtailed economic activities across China. In response to this sudden, nationwide, and potentially devastating liquidity shock, many coordinated economic and financial policies were initiated by the Chinese authorities to help the economy battle against the epidemic. In particular, policy tools have been designed to support not only industries and regions but also small- and medium-sized firms that were disproportionally hit hard by the outbreak. We then discuss the effectiveness of the policy intervention based on a series of recent surveys which cover a representative sample of public and

---

[1] zhiguo.he@chicagobooth.edu; liubb@pbcsf.tsinghua.edu.cn.

private firms. Some international comparisons are conducted, followed by discussion of the economic outlook going forward.

Liquidity Policies

* Loan Term Extension and Debt Rollover

For firms that have trouble repaying debts on time due to the COVID-19 outbreak, banks were instructed by top authorities in Beijing to extend loan terms or rollover the debts. Micro- and small-sized firms, and firms in Hubei were allowed to postpone repayment dates to June 30. As of March 22, according to the China Banking and Insurance Regulation Commission (CBIRC), around 20% of loans borrowed by micro-, small-, and medium-sized firms have been extended. By the end of March, the terms of loans worth 880 billion yuan have been extended, and loans worth 576.8 billion yuan have been rolled over. Penalty interests on overdue payments were exempted, and overdue debt caused by the outbreak would not be counted as a default (to avoid any negative impact on a firm's credit record).

In the corporate bond market, the China Securities Regulatory Commission (CSRC) supported firms with normal operation, by relaxing the restrictions on issuing new bonds that repay maturing debts.

Similarly, individuals were allowed to defer the repayments of personal loans (e.g., mortgages and credit card bills) and renegotiate interest rates. The terms of entrepreneurship loans taken out by individuals infected by the coronavirus could be extended by another year.

On the side of banks, in March the People's Bank of China (PBOC) cut the required reserve ratio of some commercial lenders, a monetary policy tool frequently used by China, to release 550 billion yuan to the real economy. Other regulatory requirements were also loosened to encourage commercial lenders to support their borrowers; for example, debts overdue for more than ninety days are no longer required to be classified as nonperforming loans.

* Share Pledge Term Extension

By the end of 2019, 40.5% of publicly listed firms in China had share pledge loans — i.e., shareholders borrowing money from other institutions (banks, trust companies, or security firms) using their floating shares as collateral. The liquidity pressure on these share pledge loans — with an outstanding amount of about 2 trillion yuan at that time — is enormous. To cope with this pressure, the CSRC has allowed shareholders in Hubei to delay the repayment of share pledge loans to security firms by 6 months; the extension period in other provinces was 3–6 months. The CBIRC made similar arrangements on shares pledged to banks and trust companies.

Financial Policies

- The Special Relending Program

On February 7, the PBOC set up a special "relending" program to provide low-interest loans to a group of shortlisted firms who are on the frontlines of the battle against the coronavirus (e.g., firms involved in the production, transport, and sales of epidemic-related medical supplies and daily necessities). According to the program, 300 billion yuan of funding from the PBOC was made available; it is termed as "relending" because the central bank first lends to various commercial banks that then lend to these shortlisted firms.

The list of these favored "frontline" firms was mainly drawn up by the National Development and Reform Commission (NDRC) and the Ministry of Industry and Information Technology (MIIT), which included more than 1,600 large companies. Another ten hand-picked provincial and municipal governments were also allowed to compile their own lists of "frontline" firms. Though the names of "frontline" firms are not publicly disclosed, a significant number of privately owned enterprises made the shortlist.

In terms of pricing, the PBOC put a ceiling of 100 bps below the prevailing one-year national LPR on the interest rates, and the Ministry of Finance (MoF) subsidized 50% of the borrowing cost. With these joint efforts, Beijing is pledging to cut the actual borrowing cost so that it is below 1.6% while the prevailing one-year LPR is about 4%. In practice, the cost is only 1.26% for loans made to 5,881 firms before the end of March, based on the statistics released by the CBIRC.

- The Increased Relending and Rediscount Quota

Soon after establishing the 300-billion-yuan special relending program, the PBOC increased relending and rediscount quotas to banks by 500 billion yuan. Local banks were allowed to obtain funds from the central bank, and then extend loans to small- and medium-sized firms, the agricultural industry, and farmers using a market-based approach — in particular, there was no a shortlist of "frontline" firms. With this initiative, loans of 276.8 billion yuan with average borrowing cost below 4.55% have been extended to 351.4 thousand borrowers as of the end of March. On March 31, the PBOC, following the instructions from the State Council, further increased the quota by 1 trillion yuan.

- Special Loans For Micro- and Small-Sized Firms

At the end of February, the CBIRC instructed banks to extend more loans at favorable rates to micro- and small-sized firms that are privately owned after the outbreak. Specifically, the largest five state-owned banks will increase their loans to small firms by 30% in the first half of 2020, and three policy banks (the China Development Bank, the Export-Import Bank of China, and the Agricultural Development Bank of China) would also make special loans of 350 billion yuan to these firms.

- Relaxed Regulations on Seasoned Equity Offering (SEOs)

In February 2020, the CSRC significantly revised the regulations on SEOs in the stock market to encourage equity financing. The SEO requirements for listed firms on the ChiNext market were considerably loosened, allowing more growth firms to raise capital. The restrictions on private placement of SEOs (e.g., pricing, lockup periods, number of investors) were also partially lifted.

Fiscal Policies

- Tax, Fee and Rent Cuts

To support firms and individuals in the wake of economic paralysis, the MoF, the State Taxation Administration (STA), the General Administration of Customs (GAC), the NDRC, and local governments set out a series of cuts and extensions in tax, social security payments, and fees. They include the following (though not an exhaustive list):

i. Most social welfare contribution paid by firms (pension, unemployment and vocational injury insurance) was exempted for up to

5 months for micro-, small-, and medium-sized firms, firms in Hubei, and self-employed business owners; and more than half of unemployment insurance premia were refunded if these firms kept all their workers. Payments by large firms were cut by half. The exemptions amounted to 123.9 billion yuan for February and are expected to exceed 500 billion yuan by June, according to the Ministry of Human Resources and Social Security.

ii. Rents owed by micro-, small-sized firms and self-employed business owners to state-owned properties were waived for 3 months.

iii. Tariffs were exempted for the import of medicines, medical supplies, and other vehicles used to fight against the outbreak.

iv. From March to May, Value-Added-Taxes for small-scale taxpayers in Hubei were exempted, and the tax rate was cut from 3% to 1% in other regions.

v. Road tolls were exempted; some service fees charged by ports, airports and railways were cut by 20%; and the price of electricity was cut by 5%.

Among these policy initiatives, the waiver on employers' welfare contributions (which roughly amount to around 15% of wages) and the exempted rents owed to State-Owned Enterprises are the most significant relieving measure for the enterprise sector. Because the coronavirus outbreak disrupted most existing businesses, reductions on Value-Added-Taxes as well as utility overheads bring only negligible benefits to most of firms.

- Payment Period Extensions

Deadlines of tax and fee payments were generally negotiable and extended; the STA extended February's statutory tax filing deadline to February 28, and these deadlines could be further extended by local tax authorities (and most of them have been extended). Additionally, firms were allowed to defer their social security payments by 6 months, and the due date for contributing to the "housing provident fund" was extended to June 30.

Discussions

In summary, thanks to coordinated efforts from many government agencies, China's economic and financial policies during the epidemic period were aggressive and targeted to help infected entrepreneurs/individuals, smaller firms, regions in trouble, and firms directly involved in providing supplies to the battle. But are there any concerns about these polices, and are the policies effective? How do they compare to that of international counterparts?

- The Impacts On the Banking Sector

Commercial banks played an important role in executing the liquidity and financing policies against the outbreak. However, it seems that these policies may hurt bank profitability and in turn the stability of the entire banking sector, because

 i. Deferred repayments, loan term extensions, and rollovers may disturb the banks' operation cycles and require additional effort for liquidity and asset management;
 ii. Exemptions for penalty interests hurt revenues; and
iii. Borrowers will be influenced by national or local authorities in many cases (e.g., the shortlisted firms in the special relending program).

We believe these policy-driven initiatives have reasonable economic motivations. The value of bank assets depends on borrowers' survivals and future earnings. Facing the unprecedented liquidity shock due to the coronavirus, banks would find it in their own interest to scarify some short-term profits to help their temporarily troubled clients survive the crisis — banks can collect deferred repayments once their client firms resume their normal operations. In fact, similar exemptions by banks have also been observed in the US without too many policy interventions.

More importantly, top policymakers in Beijing are aware of this issue, and we have mentioned several such policy supports received by commercial banks. Along this line, banks were also encouraged by the PBOC to issue perpetual bonds to raise capital. To boost the liquidity of perpetual bonds, the PBOC conducted central bank bills swaps of 21 billion yuan from February to April, with which dealers in the open market could exchange perpetual bonds for more liquid central bank bills.

- Policy Effectiveness and Challenges on Unemployment

Tsinghua PBCSF and the CSRC conducted a joint survey in late February 2020, which covered all 3,801 listed firms and 605 representative private firms. From the survey, the top five supporting policies favored by these firms are i) tax cuts and deferrals; ii) looser monetary policies; iii) loan term extensions and rollovers; iv) cutting and deferring social security payments; and v) cutting interest and deferring payments. We note that all these preferences are exactly what the top authorities in Beijing are doing. Furthermore, more than 70% of surveyed firms mentioned that they had received some help (e.g., a tax cut) from local governments, suggesting an effective and timely enforcement of the aforementioned policies.

Looking forward, though the spread of the coronavirus has been effectively contained inside China, China's economic recovery faces a mounting challenge, notwithstanding the deteriorating pandemic situation across the globe. The statistics on the macro economy in China show that on a year-to-year basis, the industrial value-added dropped by 4.3% and 25.9% in January and February, respectively. In contrast, the unemployment rate increased by 1% from 5.2% to 6.2% in February 2020 compared to December 2019.

These numbers seem to suggest that Chinese firms were largely paralyzed during the first quarter in 2020, but did not cut their labor forces. However, the joint Tsinghua PBCSF-CSRC survey showed that 60.1% firms have cash to sustain operation for three months or more. That is, they are able to maintain the current level of employment for about three months before exhausting their financial resources. If the pandemic continues for more than three months, and if there is not enough follow-on policy support, these firms may get into trouble, causing a more severe economic downturn.

- An International Comparison

Many policy tools used by major economies to battle against the pandemic are similar to those adopted by the Chinese authorities in nature. Generally, more funds are injected into the economy to support firms and households. For example, in the US, besides loosening money supply, the Federal Reserve and Department of Treasury jointly established programs to provide 300 billion dollars in new financing. A forgivable loan program of 350 billion dollars was also designed to help small enterprises' payroll for their employees. On April 21, the US Senate passed a $484 billion interim relief package as replenishment. Germany set up a 600 billion-euro rescue fund to support troubled firms with loans, guarantees and equity investments.

Fiscal policies in terms of tax cuts or deferrals are also widely used, and tax deferrals are often preferred. For instance, the US government postponed the April 15 tax payments for 90 days for individuals and firms. The UK exempted business property taxes for 12 months for the retail, leisure, and tourism sectors, and deferred 30 billion pounds in Value-Added-Tax payments to June 30.

Last but not least, outside China, governments are more engaged in providing direct subsidies to workers. The US government sent one-time 1,200-dollar direct payments to adults earning up to 75,000 dollars per annum. Britain gave 25,000 pounds to each firm hit hard by the coronavirus, and 10,000 pounds each to small businesses. Japan gave firms 8,330 yen per employee to retain workers from February 27 to May 6. The Danish government promised that firms hit by the pandemic could get aid to pay 75% of salaries, lasting for three months.

The lack of massive worker-favored polices in Beijing's responses has been criticized by many economists, but these criticisms overlook the fact that State-Owned-Enterprises in China are providing a financial safety-net for (a significant fraction of) Chinese workers. Furthermore, workers of privately owned enterprises are paid with some legally binding minimum furlough wage, as the employers face hefty severance penalties during that period. From this perspective, Beijing's aggressive firm-favored subsidy polices mentioned above also help workers, in the same spirit as the Pay-Check Protection Program in the United States. Just like their counterparts in other countries around the world, small entrepreneurs and self-employed workers in the small- and micro-business sector are the biggest losers during this pandemic lockdown.

Another interesting point, which is specific to China, is that households tend to have savings for unexpected rainy days; this effectively bought some time for the Chinese government to launch a bigger wave of subsidies during its recovery phase starting in April. This fact also helps explain why, instead of subsidies in cash like other Western governments have given, a few local governments have been partnering with private companies to send coupons to residents to boost consumption. By April 27, there were 42 cities sending 6.5 billion yuan in coupons to local residents. The reason is simple: Given the relatively high propensity of saving in China, it is more effective to encourage consumption and hence stimulate the economy in a more direct way.

- Looking Forward

China just recorded its worst quarterly GDP growth of −6.8% in 2020 Q1 since quarterly data began to be made available in 1992. The economic impact of COVID-19 on China is large, severe, and is still mounting despite various massive economic and financial policies that have been rolled out by top authorities in Beijing in a timely fashion. The situation seems to be recovering inside China, to some extent. Another more recent Tsinghua PBCSF-CSRC joint survey conducted on March 27 showed 71.4% of the listed firms had resumed more than 80% of their production capacities by then. The official unemployment rate went down by 0.3% to 5.9% at the end of March, although it is widely acknowledged that actual unemployment in China is likely to be worse than the official statistics suggest.

However, China is still facing a daunting challenge for its economic recovery at this point, especially because the deteriorating pandemic situation across the globe is bringing an almost complete halt to the export sector in China (according to the March 27 survey, 43.5% of the listed firms expect declines in 2020 overseas revenues), and could make it difficult for Chinese firms to access critical inputs provided by firms outside of China. As expected, on March 27, Beijing decided to roll out a multi-trillion-yuan stimulus package, with a refreshed focus on "new infrastructure," with much uncertainty going forward.

© 2020 World Scientific Publishing Company
https://doi.org/10.1142/9789811229381_0010

Chapter 10

Policy Rx for the Economy: Cash or Credit?

Deborah Lucas

*MIT Golub Center for Finance and Policy, Massachusetts
Institute of Technology*[1]

What is the best mix of cash and credit assistance to combat the economic fallout from the coronavirus pandemic, and what are the principles that should guide those choices? For policymakers to be able to design effective and affordable policies and avoid unintended consequences, it is essential that they understand the tradeoffs between these two broad policy alternatives. Yet this issue is rarely addressed head-on.

This is the first of a two-part series on the policy choice between cash and credit assistance. It describes the tradeoffs, and sets out a set of principles to help evaluate credit policies and the features that are likely to make them more or less effective. The second installment will apply these ideas to an analysis of the likely efficacy and cost of key provisions in the $2.2 trillion stimulus package, and the implications for future rounds of support. Even the headline number of $2.2 trillion that is arrived at by

---

[1] Sloan Distinguished Professor of Finance, Director of MIT Golub Center for Finance and Policy. This blog post first appeared on the MIT Golub Center for Finance and Policy's website, http://gcfp.mit.edu/policy-rx-for-the-economy-cash-or-credit/.

adding cash and credit support demonstrates the general lack of awareness of these two very different policy choices.

A policy is best assessed relative to desired objectives. For the policies being adopted by legislatures and central banks to combat the economic effects of the coronavirus, I take the main objectives to be (1) tiding over individuals through this period of drastically reduced incomes so as to address immediate hardships and cover basic needs; (2) providing continuity and preventing permanent damage to individual livelihoods and organizational capital; (3) bolstering the resources available to the health-care system; and (4) achieving policy objectives as cost-effectively as possible and in ways that are perceived as fair.

Cash assistance has several advantages over credit for addressing (1), (2), and (3). Cash almost always reaches the targeted recipients. It can be distributed quickly, through existing channels with little new bureaucracy. It is transparent who gets how much (with some notable exceptions when agencies are granted wide latitude on how money will be spent).

On the downside, cash assistance is expensive; it adds dollar for dollar to a federal debt that was on its way to being unsustainable long before the current crisis hit. Relatedly, the subsidy element of cash tends to be significantly higher than for credit. Subsidies, particularly large ones, raise concerns about fairness and unwarranted handouts to favored industries or constituencies.

Well-constructed credit programs can avoid or at least mitigate some of the drawbacks to cash assistance, but credit is not a silver bullet.

Like cash, credit can provide funds to tide households or businesses over spells of reduced income. When banks and other private financial institutions cut back on risky lending, or when borrowers no longer meet the normal credit standards, governments can step in with direct loans and credit guarantees.

The cost to the government is often quite low relative to the amount of funds that are made available, making it a cost-effective way to get money into the hands of people and businesses during times of crisis when liquidity is scarce. That's because most of the money, including accumulated interest, is likely to be eventually repaid. Further, the obligation to repay debt makes it more credible that those that choose to borrow have a worthwhile use for the funds. (A detailed analysis exploring the power that government credit had as relatively inexpensive stimulus during the period following the 2008 financial crisis can be found in my Brookings Paper.)[2]

Turning to some of the important principles for understanding and effectively implementing credit programs, here is my list (see also subsequent paragraphs for additional discussion):

(1) A forbearance policy for existing credit obligations will have fundamentally different effects than a policy that offers newly available federally-backed credit.

(2) Forbearance has most of the advantages of cash grants in terms of the speed of getting money out and target efficiency. At the same time, it has a lower cost than cash assistance.

(3) Removing impediments to refinancing federally-backed mortgages and other federal loans frees up cash by lowering the size of fixed monthly payments. Such policies also have a relatively low cost to taxpayers.

(4) In terms of cost, forgiving principal or interest is equivalent to directly providing cash. It is typically much less effective as a source of funds than either forbearance or cash assistance because reduced balances generally have little or no effect on current payment obligations.

(5) Creating new credit programs or expanding existing ones entails considerable uncertainty about utilization rates, and administrative and subsidy costs can be significant.

(6) Many potential borrowers will be reluctant to incur new debt obligations, even at a zero or negative interest rates, during a time of great uncertainty. Businesses cannot be expected to borrow unless it is clearly in their best interest to do so.

(7) A credit program with a very high default rate may be more costly to taxpayers than a cash program that provides similar amounts of funding when administrative costs including for collecting on defaulted loans is factored in. High-risk loans can also be harmful to the borrowers themselves as defaults hurt future credit and foreclosures on homes can be traumatic.

---

[2] Lucas Deborah. (2016). *Credit Policy as Fiscal Policy* [PDF file]. Retrieved from https://www.brookings.edu/wp-content/uploads/2016/03/lucastextspring16bpea.pdf.

(8) Finally, the budgetary treatment of credit in the US systematically understates its cost to taxpayers relative to cash assistance, creating a budgetary incentive to over-rely on credit assistance. This does not negate the advantages of credit over cash in some instances, but it is a caution against believing that credit is often a free lunch, as budget estimates too often conclude.

Forbearance involves changing the terms of existing loans so that payments can be fully or partially postponed for a period of time, such as during a layoff or spell of unemployment. Missed payments are generally added to the loan balance, along with accrued interest. Those larger balances mean that eventually payments will be higher, but by spreading the increase over the remaining life of the loan the future burden can be minimized. Forbearance can be combined with partial forgiveness, as is currently done with income-based repayment for student loans, to avoid unaffordable debt burdens.

Through its mortgage, student loan, small business, agricultural, emergency and other lending programs, the federal government is the largest provider of credit to US households. Many of those programs already allow for forbearance in the event of a crisis.

Using its power to forbear provides the US government with a powerful mechanism for quickly reducing the cash needs for the many tens of millions of citizens with mortgages, student loans, and other types of federal credit. Exercising forbearance would also contribute to the goal of minimizing longer term damage to individuals and the economy by avoiding defaults that would damage credit scores. That would not only preserve future access to credit, but it would also improve employment prospects.

The costs of such federal forbearance would likely be modest. Unless the economy has a much more protracted downturn than most experts are predicting, the ultimate default rate may be only slightly higher than it otherwise would have been. However, when forbearance is combined with forgiveness of principal or interest, the cost for that portion of the assistance rises to be equivalent to that of direct cash grants.

Extending new credit through expanded or newly implemented programs has much less predictable effects than forbearance or easing restrictions on refinancing. For example, there have been calls to lend to businesses so that they can continue to pay furloughed or underemployed workers. Borrowing for that purpose would put the business at risk to default, and it seems unlikely that the take-up rate for such a program would save a lot of jobs.

© 2020 World Scientific Publishing Company
https://doi.org/10.1142/9789811229381_0011

Chapter 11

The State as Insurer of Last Resort

Joseph Cherian* and Bernard Yeung[†,1]

*NUS Business School, National University of Singapore
†NUS Business School, National University of Singapore;
Asian Bureau of Finance and Economic Research

Finance 101

Arrow–Debreu (A–D) securities, which were postulated in the 1950s, demonstrate how in complete markets any payoff structure can be obtained by a linear combination of the underlying "pure" A–D securities. Put simply, state-contingent contracts with arbitrary payoff structures could be constructed to allow investors to hedge or insure against any undesirable outcome, state of nature and/or aggregate risk.

In some cases, systematic risks can be insured or hedged against, for example by using put options (futures) on the S&P 500 to insure (hedge) against market declines, or catastrophic bonds in the event of natural disasters.

---

[1] Joseph Cherian is Practice Professor of Finance at Singapore's NUS Business School, while Bernard Yeung is the President of the Asian Bureau of Finance and Economic Research (ABFER) and the Stephen Riady Distinguished Professor in Finance and Strategic Management at NUS Business School.

In other cases — either due to market breakdowns or the inability of the market to bear all the associated risks from a cost, institutional or regulatory perspective — this is not possible. Say, in the case of inflation or pandemic disease risk. In such circumstances, the state has a distinctive role to play as the insurer of last resort.

The world is now facing a pandemic of catastrophic health and economic consequences globally. To break the chain of the coronavirus transmission and mitigate the attendant public health threat — commonly known as "flattening the contagion curve" (most akin to a Central Bank's yield curve flattening exercise by pursuing unconventional monetary policy) — almost all countries are imposing lockdowns to reduce human mobility and face-to-face interactions. Yet, many economic activities rely on just that.

The vigilant measures have generated a huge negative supply and demand shock and disrupted global production value-chains and trade greatly. The consequence is a significant decline in output, surge in unemployment, bankruptcy, and worries over financial stability. Many have remarked that the current economic setback is more serious than the Global Financial Crisis the world experienced in 2008–2009, while a few have postulated it could be as bad as the Great Depression of the 1930s.

As we know from the economic tradeoff literature, there is also no free lunch in business and finance. Every action taken by governments to stem the spread of the virus has an economic cost. Some economic sectors have effectively shut down during this pandemic, taking a toll on incomes, jobs, growth and even inter-nation goodwill and policy coordination. The policy question is how we can sustain the economy *ad interim* so that it can recover and thrive when the virus pandemic is behind us.

A financial market analogue would be useful. During periods of extreme stress, Treasury markets have been known to go helter-skelter in prices, for example, when there's a technical squeeze on a particular Treasury bond. This will result in its price rising to an abnormally high level temporarily. Let's assume investor A was massively short the bond prior to the squeeze occurring. Margin calls during the temporary elevation in price could overwhelm the liquidity condition or solvency of A in the *short run*, even though A's short position could have been the right call in the *long run*. In the extreme case, it could lead to A's bankruptcy.

However, if a deep-pocketed government fund comes to A's rescue by providing the necessary liquidity to tide A over the difficult (yet short run) "squeeze period" in exchange for equity, or the government reopens that particular Treasury issue to alleviate the squeeze, investor A could survive, recover and potentially thrive in the long run. In other words, when markets break down, be it due to a technical squeeze on Treasuries, a terrorist attack or a global pandemic, and there isn't any way to hedge against it using the equivalent of A–D securities, the government must step in and provide the necessary relief.

The Point

Thus, there is theoretical justification for the state to undertake responsibility to insure its members against exogenous systemic negative shocks. Rescue plans are plentiful, and Singapore's plans have the hallmarks of most rescue plans. We use, by way of illustration, Singapore's rescue plans to date, which amounts to about 12% of its gross domestic product. In addition to bolstering the resources available to the healthcare system given this is a pandemic, Singapore's plans include these essential features:

a. addressing individuals' immediate hardships and covering their basic needs;
b. mitigating job market disruptions and preventing permanent damage to businesses' organizational capital, particularly those in the hard-hit industries like transportation, tourism, retail and restaurants;
c. maintaining market-wide financial stability and individual financial security, mostly via forbearance programs, interest and principal payment deferrals, and contractual obligation temporary relief.

Cash, and Hurry!

First, there was the express delivery of cash into Singaporeans' bank accounts starting in mid-April 2020, with more help given to the lower income. Why targeted cash handouts? A carefully calibrated and targeted cash scheme would be advantageous for both the individuals and the economy. Research shows students, lower-income households, and retirees on fixed incomes spend cash gifts more quickly. This is because they need cash the most, especially during a sudden exigency, and hence spend it the fastest. Additionally, the expeditious manner of their spending helps stabilize the economy the quickest. This double-happiness effect stems from such a policy.

To this point, the Singapore government in its recent Budget 2020, introduced a series of carefully targeted cash payouts, workfare special payments, grocery and sales vouchers, and rebates on service and conservancy charges (a form of homeowners' association fee), particularly for the lower-income households and self-employed.

Flatteners, Forbearance and Force Majeure

Second, as part of the COVID-19 financial support program for individuals and households, various governments also offered mortgage and interest payment relief through the suspension of mortgage payments itself or refinancing opportunities from interest rate cuts and tax holidays.

In Singapore, the central bank announced that qualifying individuals can apply to defer both principal and interest repayment of residential property loans, while small- and medium-sized enterprises (SME) can defer principal payments on secured term loans up until year end. They can also apply to defer payments on health and life insurance programs for up to six months, and tax payments by three months.

The Singapore Ministry of Law is also proposing a law that provides "temporary relief from legal action — on a just and equitable basis — to individuals and businesses who are unable to fulfil their contractual obligations due to COVID-19". This relief would be for a period of up to six months, and extendable for another six. Such a state-led measure first-order dominates a scenario where companies independently declare *force majeure* during this pandemic period.

Any extra spending money in an individual's pocket from the package is not going to be a game-changer for household savings and investments. It is meant more to tide people over this difficult and turbulent period. That said, having various private and state-provisioned "insurance" policies, be it for health, unemployment, disability, death, stock market crashes or pandemics, is always important, in both normal and turbulent times.

Save the Jobs and Organizational Capital

Third, saving jobs is important. As a quick-sighted New York Times editorial pointed out on March 26, 2020, *"Preserving jobs is important because a job isn't merely about the money. Compensated labor provides a sense of independence, identity and purpose; an unemployment check does not replace any of those things. Additionally, a substantial body of research on earlier economic downturns documents that people who lose jobs, even if they eventually find new ones, suffer lasting damage to their earnings potential, health and even the prospects of their children."*

Singapore has indeed stepped up to the plate on the employment front by asking employers not to resort to layoffs and no-pay leaves. To motivate employers in that direction, the government paid out 75% of all local employees' wages for the local lockdown month of April, with 25% coverage for another eight months after that, with much higher subsidies — up to 75% — for the sectors most affected by this pandemic. This includes employers' contributions to the mandatory social security savings scheme.

This program, essentially a temporary subsidy, incentivizes companies not to break up their human capital or work teams, and possibly cleverly deploy them for other meaningful activities such as problem-solving for the company's operational stresses due to lockdown measures.

Stabilization and support extend beyond mitigating job losses. It includes economy-wide measures to help businesses survive the undue pressures on cash flows arising from an exogenous systemic shock; this is like insuring investment on building organizational capital. The Singapore's package offers property tax and corporate income tax rebates, waiver of government rental charges, and bridge loans to cover short term cash shortfalls.

Respect and Tech for Elders

Fourth, the impact of the pandemic is particularly severe on senior care and the savings of retirees.

Asia in general and Singapore, in particular, faces an ageing population. The death rate of the infected is disproportionately high for seniors. Note, however, elder care, housing, nursing homes and retirement facilities have been gaining popularity in ageing Asia regions. The deadly experience of the Seattle-area nursing homes to COVID-19 may change the rules for elder care.

To mitigate the risk of exposing the elderly to COVID-19, serving them requires less reliance on human mobility, where caregivers, entertainers, volunteers and healthcare workers deploy in multiple locations. Instead, there should be more dependence on dedicated teams, technology and faster response times during crises. The Singapore government suspended seniors' social activities and encourages institutions involved in elder care to replace physical visits with technologies such as teleconferencing via smartphones to both help the elderly become digitally-savvy and to lead more independent and empowered lives.

The trend has to be sustained. Transforming elder care habits, systems and infrastructure to the new world order require asset owners' patient capital and participation. Pension plans and sovereign funds with socially responsible investment motivations may be the natural long-term capital provider or partner for this transformation.

Last but not least, the pandemic-induced global economic stress greatly erodes the principal and earnings of seniors' savings. The Singapore government took bold steps to raise the "silver support" (support to the retired) by 20%.

Post-Pandemonium Coordination

Financial economics is an applied science that deals with the intertemporal allocation of scarce resources under conditions of uncertainty and unexpected shocks. While a well-endowed state can come to the rescue when financial markets and products cannot, it could also cause serious problems if central banks and government funds are all rushing for the door at the same time raising funds to finance their massive stimulus packages. It would be a fire-sale of the most liquid — and probably most highly correlated — assets of unimaginable proportions.

Which brings us to our concluding thought. Since the COVID-19 disease is a global problem, some form of multilateral policy coordination is necessary for humanity to succeed in lifting us out of this pandemic as well as for economies to recover. While there are reports of the IMF providing credit lines for poorer nations, or a few central banks arranging for bilateral currency swap lines to ease the virus-related strains on credit markets and provide US dollar liquidity to financial institutions, there is an urgent call-to-action for right-minded political leaders to do much more — systematically and on the global coordination front. At this juncture, it is paramount that the two most powerful nations on this earth join hands to promote international cooperation, a wish we harbor for humanity's sake. Unfortunately, the opposite is happening, which will aggravate the world's suffering.

On the bright side, every global crisis presents opportunities for our collective learning, to alleviate suffering amongst the lower-income groups and SMEs, and to generally improve financial economic outcomes while maximizing social welfare.

© 2020 World Scientific Publishing Company
https://doi.org/10.1142/9789811229381_0012

Chapter 12

Singapore's Policy Response to COVID-19[1]

Danny Quah

*Lee Kuan Yew School of Public Policy,
National University of Singapore*

This chapter describes Singapore's economic policy response to the 2020 COVID-19 outbreak. Although the core interest in this discussion is economic, two companion attributes in the suite of Singapore's policies feature prominently. The first concerns trust in political leadership; the second, confidence in technical competence and scientific expertise.

This chapter argues that it is the coming together of these three — economic policy, assured political leadership, and expert evidence-based domain knowledge — that has made for Singapore's thus-far successful response to the COVID-19 outbreak.

(Following the World Health Organization convention,[2] I will refer to COVID-19 for the disease but to the virus itself by a different name, SARS-CoV-2 or the novel coronavirus, or when there's no ambiguity, just coronavirus.)

---

[1] *This article was first published in CEPR Press VoxEU eBook "Mitigating the COVID Economic Crisis: Act Fast and Do Whatever It Takes".*

[2] Naming the coronavirus disease (COVID-19) and the virus that causes it. (n.d.). Retrieved August 13, 2020, from https://www.who.int/emergencies/diseases/novel-coronavirus-

Unlike a routine economic shock, with impact of perhaps up to a standard deviation on price and quantity, the introduction of the novel coronavirus into national conversation brings into focus for market participants questions of heightened social fears, not least in the form of widespread health emergencies and a collapsed healthcare system. Will COVID-19 be just about disturbances to demand and supply, or will markets — organized systems of exchange — break down altogether?

In the COVID-19 outbreak, ordinary people confront changing restrictions not just through price variations affecting the value of their endowments of time and wealth. Instead, people face quarantine-related, non-price constraints in their physical mobility and thus contend with restrictions on their labor force activity and economic production. These social engineering constraints imply further that people are restricted in leisure group engagements and thus in consumption activity. The shock to people's psychological composure — in social distancing, self-isolation, working from home — affects consumer confidence and worker efficiency.

For COVID-19, therefore, the disturbance to aggregate demand and supply come together. So too should policy respond on multiple fronts. In this view, attempting to support just aggregate demand, say, will result only in distortion and further disruption to the economy. This note therefore presents Singapore's economic policy response to COVID-19 against a background that acknowledges the multiplicity and correlatedness of COVID-19's different effects.

Elsewhere, the broad, general contours of Singapore's COVID-19 actions have already been described.[3] Some of these accounts

---

2019/technical-guidance/naming-the-coronavirus-disease-(covid-2019)-and-the-virus-that-causes-it.

[3] Barron, L. (March 13, 2020). Coronavirus lessons from Singapore, Taiwan and Hong Kong. Retrieved August 13, 2020, from https://time.com/5802293/coronavirus-covid19-singapore-hong-kong-taiwan/.

Cowling, B. and Lim, W. (March 13, 2020). They've contained the Coronavirus. Here's how. Retrieved August 13, 2020, from https://www.nytimes.com/2020/03/13/opinion/coronavirus-best-response.html.

Wells, S. (April 10, 2020). Singapore is the model for how to handle the coronavirus. Retrieved August 13, 2020, from https://www.technologyreview.com/2020/03/12/905346/singapore-is-the-model-for-how-to-handle-the-coronavirus/.

characterize Singapore as having undertaken "draconian tracing and containment measures", with its small population therefore "largely accepting of the government's expansive orders". One observer in New York noted how in a public health crisis, Singaporeans seemed to show "more of a willingness to place the community and society needs over individual liberty".

My own view is that in Singapore well-designed economic incentive schemes, working in tandem with established domestic laws and the population's confidence in scientific knowledge and political leadership, have been critical in reaching good outcomes.

The narrative that follows presents, in the main, just facts, drawing directly from material on Singapore's Ministry websites, or in first-hand accounts of speeches or other official engagement.

On January 2, 2020, Singapore's Ministry of Health (MOH) first began to issue public advisories on an emerging cluster of pneumonia cases in Wuhan, Hubei province, China. Temperature screening was set up for inbound travellers at Singapore's Changi airport the following day. The first case of COVID-19 in Singapore was confirmed on January 23, 2020. In the week between then and February 1, eighteen cases were confirmed, every single one of them connected to the case having recent physical presence in Wuhan.

In late January, both in anticipation and in response, a number of housing properties (including at the National University of Singapore) were designated Government Quarantine Facilities, to accommodate those who had been in close contact with COVID-19 confirmed cases. People who might also have been exposed but were thought to be at lower risk were placed on compulsory Leave of Absence (LOA), to be contacted regularly for health monitoring. All who were quarantined or placed on LOA were newly returned from Wuhan.

Tuesday, February 4, 2020, however, changed that discourse: The first local coronavirus transmission was detected. MOH confirmed four cases, none of whom had recently travelled to Mainland China. Three of these had had contact with recent travellers from Mainland China. The fourth had not, but was a domestic worker for one of the three. This change in circumstances took infection possibilities to a new level, with the negative impact on aggregate demand and supply growing correspondingly larger.

If up until then the strategy was one of border control, that strategy now needed to change, to containment and social distancing.

Three days after that, on Friday, February 7, Singapore's Disease Outbreak Response Condition (DORSCON) was raised from Yellow to Orange, indicating the novel coronavirus outbreak was now estimated to have moderate to high public health impact. Across the island, inessential large-scale events were cancelled or postponed. Universities and businesses put up thermal screening stations, and twice-daily temperature reporting by every individual was mandated. Soon thereafter a new category of medical isolation, Stay-Home Notification (SHN), was introduced, in severity between a Quarantine Order (QO) and an LOA. Both QO and SHN attract the full force of the law under the Infectious Diseases Act, and so carry legal penalty.

Economic Policy

On economics, first, context and a sense of magnitude: Singapore is a small open economy that trades in a typical year between three to four times its total GDP. In 2019 that total GDP stood at S$508 billion, having grown that year at a 0.7% annual rate, down from 2018's 3.4%. (On December 15, 2019, S$1 was worth US$0.74, so Singapore's 2019 GDP amounted to US$376 billion or US$66,000 per capita.)

In November 2019, Singapore's Ministry of Trade and Industry (MTI) officially forecast that 2020 GDP growth would fall within the range 0.5% to 2.5%.

The COVID-19 outbreak swiftly changed that. MTI *revised down its 2020 forecast interval to −0.5% to 1.5%*, i.e., by a full one percentage point within the space of, essentially, weeks.[4] This assessment was conditioned on expected weaker growth in China, but keeping broadly unchanged the 2020 outlook for the US and Eurozone economies.

From the perspective of March 2020, China's growth would likely continue to be low even if COVID-19 containment appeared to have been successful unexpectedly and quickly. However, in the weeks since the

---

[4] Subhani, O. and Tan, S. (February 17, 2020). Singapore downgrades 2020 economic growth forecast to between −0.5% and 1.5% on coronavirus impact. Retrieved August 13, 2020, from https://www.straitstimes.com/business/economy/singapore-downgrades-2020-economic-growth-forecast-to-05-15-on-coronavirus-impact.

MTI's February assessment, the US and Eurozone economies began to look distinctly weaker than thought then to be the case. Moreover, COVID-19's economic impact, not just on the US or the Eurozone but globally, will probably be larger than previously expected.

If the lower end of MTI's February forecast range materializes, 2020 will be a full one-year period of negative growth in Singapore, the first since 2001. Even the 2003 SARS outbreak *reduced GDP by 0.3% for just one quarter*, and afterwards saw record GDP expansion of 5.3% in the quarter that followed.

The predicted impact of the COVID-19 outbreak on Singapore's economy, therefore, is larger than any other event of the last two decades, including the 2008 Global Financial Crisis.

Second, what has been the economic policy response?

The economic policies that have been applied can be divided, logically, into those formed within the 2020 Government Budget process (coincidentally announced in February 2020), and those constituted outside that process.

We begin with the second category: with the COVID-19 outbreak leading to a range of quarantine-derived restrictions imposed on business and workers, the Government quickly realized that, all else equal, the incentive was for even the ill and infected to keep going in to the work-place. The externality this inflicts is that those otherwise healthy around the sick colleague experience an increased risk that they too will fall ill. So, by mid-February the Government had put in place *a scheme to help compensate businesses and the self-employed for those under COVID-19 Leave of Absence*. Although the compensation is not 100% this is a move towards guaranteeing paid sick leave.

Along the same lines of externality management, COVID-19 testing is free, although those suspecting infection but not yet showing respiratory symptoms are encouraged to practise just self-isolation and social distancing.

We turn now to the 2020 Government Budget. Tuesday, February 18 was when Singapore's Finance Minister Heng Swee Keat was scheduled to present the Budget to Parliament.

To appreciate better the significance of this Budget, we should note two facts. First, by then the name COVID-19 was only a week old. Second, Singapore's Government operates on a *principle of budget balance over each term of Government*. Thus, for instance, from 2001 to 2010, a period that includes the 2008 Global Financial Crisis, Singapore's overall Budget Balance averaged to +0.1% of GDP.

The 2020 Budget, by contrast, showed an expected deficit of S$10.9 billion, fully 2% of GDP, with total spending by Ministries amounting to S$83.6 billion. This deficit exceeds the S$8.7 billion of the 2009 Budget during the Global Financial Crisis, although in relative terms 2009's did come to 3.2% of GDP.

Included in this unusual Government expenditure is a S$4 billion **Stabilisation and Support package**[5] targeted specifically at COVID-19 issues. The ingredients of the package provide support on both aggregate demand and supply:

- Jobs Support Scheme, S$1.3 billion, where the Government pays 8% of the wages of local workers for 3 months, up to a S$3,600 monthly cap. Singapore has 1.9 million local workers;
- Wage Credit Scheme, S$1.1 billion, where the Government co-funds approximately 20% wage increases for Singaporean employees, up to a S$5,000 gross monthly wage (the exact parameters taper over time);
- Care and Support Package, S$1.6 billion, where the Government provides one-off cash payments of between S$100 to S$300 to every Singaporean aged 21 or higher, thus helping households defray the cost of living.

Beyond these large components, the 2020 Budget also includes corporate income tax rebates of up to 25% of total tax payable in 2020; faster write-down for investment incurred in 2021; government co-financing on working capital loans; increased flexibility in rental payments for commercial enterprises on government properties; and re-training and re-skilling programmes for staff in tourism, transport, and other affected sectors.

In comparison with fiscal spending on average in history, the scale and extent of this expansionary and support policy are remarkable. The policy is targeted, moreover, with the most vulnerable and affected in the Singapore economy receiving greater but still time-limited attention. Both demand and supply side considerations are taken into account: Businesses receive investment relief at the same time that consumers see immediate boost to cash holdings, thus raising economy-wide spending power.

---

[5] MOF: Singapore Budget 2020: Home. (n.d.). Retrieved August 13, 2020, from https://www.singaporebudget.gov.sg/budget_2020.

Further, in February the Monetary Authority of Singapore, the nation's central bank, announced that it was "prepared to recalibrate monetary policy" if the economic outlook deteriorated further.

At the end of February, to show solidarity with other Singaporeans coping with the coronavirus outbreak, the President of the Republic of Singapore, the Prime Minister, all Cabinet Ministers, and all political office-holders took a one-month pay cut. The Finance Minister, at the same time, announced that healthcare frontline workers would receive an extra month's special bonus.

Finally, in his March 12 speech, the Prime Minister, Lee Hsien Loong, added to what had been in the Finance Minister's Budget, by announcing that, as needed, the Government was already putting together a second package of support measures to continue to help businesses, workers, and households.

Technical Knowledge and Scientific Expertise

Beyond economics, Singapore's other domain experts have approached the challenge of this pandemic in a way that has, by all accounts, continued to build trust among Singaporeans.

Throughout January, even as the first isolated, imported COVID-19 cases were being confirmed, MOH maintained clear, consistent, and informative messaging on their website. In the evening of every day, the current state of confirmed cases would be reported, normally with precise information on where the confirmed cases had travelled, and continuing updates on individuals with whom the various confirmed cases had come in contact. Singaporeans could develop a clear picture for themselves what was happening with COVID-19 across the nation.

Within a week of the first confirmed case in Singapore, researchers at Duke-NUS (National University of Singapore) announced they had *cultured the novel coronavirus* from a patient's clinical sample, thus aiding the development of new diagnostic methods and the testing of potential vaccines.[6]

When spatial clusters of COVID-19 concentration emerged, MOH and affiliated agencies painstakingly undertook contact tracing until practically every individual was accounted for. Again, Duke-NUS developed a crucial

---

[6]Wuhan Coronavirus: Scientists in Singapore culture virus from patient. (n.d.). Retrieved August 13, 2020, from https://www.duke-nus.edu.sg/allnews/media-releases/wuhan-coronavirus.

new serological test able to establish links across infected individuals, even when, after recovery, a patient had cleared the virus from their system.[7] This was put to use to connect up two previously distinct clusters in Singapore, clarifying the transmission mechanism and identifying the individuals who had served to link the clusters.

That Singaporeans understood why such detailed knowledge mattered and how the risks were asymmetrically distributed also helped the process of confidence-building. South Korea too had done systematic and exhaustive monitoring. Their first confirmed case was discovered on January 20, 2020: "Patient 1" had flown from Wuhan to Incheon International Airport in Seoul. Upon discovery, she was isolated. In the weeks that followed, in a city of 10 million, only 30 new cases occurred, even with "Patient 6" having contracted the virus locally. But then "Patient 31" — how she became infected remains unclear — denied she'd been told to get tested for the virus, attended service twice at the Daegu branch of the Shincheonji Church of Jesus along with 9,300 others. Within weeks *hundreds tested positive for COVID-19*, with South Korea's total cases now numbering in excess of 8,000.[8]

Singaporeans could see, transparently, the dynamic unfolding between new, carefully reported scientific evidence and corresponding policy measures taken. The same evening (Tuesday, February 4) that the first local coronavirus transmission was recorded, the Minister of Education informed that primary and secondary schools would suspend large group and communal activities. That weekend, universities, business, and most other establishments set up thermal scanning stations ahead of the coming work week.

In this environment when, say, social distancing is asked of the population, it does not take a great deal of convoluted calculation to evaluate costs and benefits, and to take on board the advice from both science and political leadership. Policies are simply that much more effective when there is trust in science.

---

[7] Normile, D. (February 27, 2020). Singapore claims first use of antibody test to track coronavirus infections. Science. Retrieved from http://www.sciencemag.org/news/2020/02/singapore-claims-first-use-antibody-test-track-coronavirus-infections/.

[8] Scarr, S., Hernandez, M. and Sharma, M. (March 12, 2020). 2019 coronavirus: The Korean clusters. Retrieved August 13, 2020, from https://graphics.reuters.com/CHINA-HEALTH-SOUTHKOREA-CLUSTERS/0100B5G33SB/index.html.

Communication and Political Leadership

The evening of Friday, February 7, 2020, after MOH announced Singapore was going into DORSCON Orange, some supermarket shelves across the island were quickly emptied, including those that notoriously should have held toilet paper.

The following day the Prime Minister, Lee Hsien Loong, went on TV to address the nation. By all accounts, the message was the very model of good communication and national leadership. The speech explained to the audience what economic and social reserves Singapore would be able to draw on, what was new in the threat posed by the novel coronavirus, what measures were in place, and how individual Singaporeans could help.

Most critically, the speech pointed to how strategies would need to be reconsidered as the situation continued to unfold, and scientific understanding grew with more data. When Singapore's Foreign Minister Vivian Balakrishnan was interviewed on CNBC on March 11, 2020, he set out how the challenge is now global and likely continuing into perhaps the next year. He described how Singapore will need to meet the challenge by working together with others, both in the region and worldwide. The approach is one where "We prepare for the worst. We get all our measures lined up, coordinated. We communicate with our people; people understand what we are doing."

In Singapore the messaging has remained clear, consistent, and well-informed. Credibility is high. This has continued to reassure the population appropriately, and maintain trust in the system. Demand and supply work best when there is confidence in social mechanisms.

Contrast this with how in the US the Trump White House went from one week boldly announcing the US would have zero cases, to the next week having to deal with more than 2,000 confirmed infections and nearly 50 deaths. The US President refused to accept responsibility for testing delays, blaming instead others inside and outside his administration. He continued to contradict his own health officials. All this has *elevated anxiety and uncertainty among Americans.*[9]

---

[9] Carolyn, Y. and Johnson, W. (March 14, 2020). Trump is breaking every rule in the CDC's 450-page playbook for health crisis. Retrieved August 13, 2020, from https://www.washingtonpost.com/health/2020/03/14/cdc-manual-crisis-coronavirus-trump/.

Even the most expansionary of monetary policy is going to face a steep challenge restoring American consumers' confidence in the face of such erratic top leadership.

The US Centers for Disease Control and Prevention (CDC) suggest a *simple formula for public health communication:* "Be consistent. Be accurate. Don't withhold vital information. Don't let anyone onto the podium without the preparation, knowledge, and discipline to deliver vital messages." If a threat is going to make many ill, don't falsely reassure them. Information that is frightening still needs to be conveyed, but do so with empathy. Help people see at an individual level what they can do to help.

Singapore's political and scientific leadership seem to have taken exactly the CDC formula to heart for their public announcements. The Trump White House, the complete opposite. One might have been tempted to say the Singapore approach is only one of good plain common sense. That the US approach has been so different suggests that there is little that is plain or common in that approach.

Conclusion

This note proposes the hypothesis that Singapore's policy response to the COVID-19 outbreak has taken three broad strands: first, economic, to repair potential falls in aggregate demand and supply, and possible market failures; second, scientific, to confront head-on the health and medical challenges, and to build confidence in the system; and third, political, with leadership showing itself in command of the situation to the greatest extent possible, and admitting the need to continue learning as knowledge gaps closed, as well as being willing to adapt policies as a result.

Each of these strands is, by itself, sensible and effective. But, additionally, they also feed off each other, and through positive spill over effects, strengthen the benefits of the policy response. In the interpretation given in this note, what has worked for Singapore is scientific and political leadership both communicating a clear understanding of the situation — identifying risks and challenges — together with economic policies that address both demand and supply considerations, and that support a continued stable social system for productive exchange.

© 2020 World Scientific Publishing Company
https://doi.org/10.1142/9789811229381_0013

Chapter 13

Singapore's Coordinated Battle Against the Pandemic

Weina Zhang and Ruth Tan

NUS Business School, National University of Singapore

Like other countries, Singapore has been affected by the pandemic; it has gone through partial lockdown, full lockdown, and has just reopened. This article reflects upon and draws learning from its experience.

Coordinated Battle

Singapore's approach is grounded on a coordinated effort of the people, the public sector and the private sector. Given that Singapore is an open and highly connected economy that is heavily reliant on international trade, collaboration and support from external parties is also key (see Figure 1). Although what Singapore does may not be unique, the holistic and comprehensive nature of the concerted and coordinated effort is exemplary.

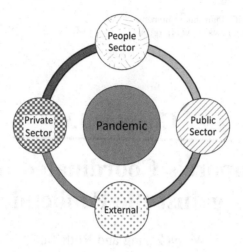

Figure 1.   Battling the pandemic together.

Public sector

Co-ordinated at the highest level

The multi-ministry task force is coordinated at the highest level with two senior ministers (Minister for National Development Lawrence Wong and Health Minister Gan Kim Yong) and the Deputy Prime Minister (Heng Swee Keat).

Community tracing

A key strategy taken by the task force is strict contact tracing in the community to ring-fence each cluster, in order to limit the spread of the virus. According to a recent study by the National Centre of Infectious Disease (NCID), contact tracing is one of the key contributing factors for the low local transmission rate in the general community. The launch of the "TraceTogether" and "OneServiceApp" mobile apps helped in identifying close contacts and enforcing better compliance respectively.

Agile

The government used a gradualism approach and reacted in an agile manner. The lockdown (termed "circuit breaker"), which started on April 7, 2020 and originally scheduled to end on May 4, 2020, was extended to June 1, 2020, with a multiple-stage re-opening arrangement. The wearing of masks became compulsory on April 14, 2020. The list of essential services was trimmed on April 21, 2020, to exclude hairdressing salons, confectioneries, and standalone beverage outlets.

The government has provided four rounds of stimulus packages totaling S$92.9 billion, the equivalent of 18.3% of 2019 GDP, focusing on care and stability, with 80% set aside for job protection, SME rescue and transformation.

- On February 18, 2020, the first "UNITY BUDGET" of S$6.4 billion was announced by Deputy Prime Minister (DPM) Heng. It was split into three categories: (1) S$4 billion Stabilization and Support Package to help businesses and workers; (2) S$1.6 billion Care and Support Package to help households deal with the cost of living; (3) S$800 million for the Ministry of Health, in addition to the annual budget, to help fight the coronavirus.
- On March 26, 2020, DPM Heng unveiled the second "RESILIENCE BUDGET" of S$48.4 billion. It had three main thrusts: (1) to save jobs and support workers; (2) help firms in the short term; and (3) strengthen long-term resilience.
- On April 7, 2020, the third "SOLIDARITY BUDGET" of S$5.1 billion was announced to help firms and families through the circuit breaker phase as workplaces closed. It included a one-off payment of S$600 for all Singaporeans aged 21 and above as well as "Jobs Support Scheme Enhanced" where the government subsidised 75% of the first S$4,600 of gross monthly wages for all 1.9 million local workers for April and 25% thereafter for a total of nine months, with a higher subsidy of 50% for food services and 75% for aviation and tourism.
- On May 26, 2020, DPM Heng announced the fourth "FORTITUDE BUDGET" worth S$33 billion to (1) help create jobs and build skills

for the workers; (2) boost transformation for enterprises; and (3) strengthen resilience for the community as the country emerged from the circuit breaker.

Repayment deferment for residential property loans

The Monetary Authority of Singapore, in collaboration with the financial industry, also put forth a relief package to help affected individuals who have difficulties meeting repayments of their mortgage loans. The initiative allows them to defer repayment of principal or both principal and interest up to December 31, 2020.

Private sector

Adaptation and innovation

Many businesses have innovated and acquired new technology and skills to overcome constraints due to social distancing measures. They have generally coped with and adapted to the new norm of e-meetings, e-conferencing, and working from home.

Corporate support

Many companies have stepped up their corporate social responsibility (CSR). Instead of raising prices, some suppliers of food and essential items have kept prices stable or even reduced them. Some have made cash and in-kind donations to the less fortunate. Some companies that could not continue operating have systematically tried to re-deploy their staff to other sectors. Some have volunteered their business spaces for quarantine purposes, their vehicles for transportation of patients, and their facilities to produce masks for local use. Some restaurants and hotels cooked and delivered meals for quarantined patients and medical staff, for free or at discounted prices. These efforts not only helped to build a sense of unity within the companies but also across other stakeholders such as suppliers, customers, government, and society at large. Public and private healthcare service providers alike actively test, treat, and care for COVID-19 patients.

People sector

The people sector, including grassroots organizations, clubs, and clan associations, provided social support and help in the distribution of free masks.

In total, the government organized distribution of free masks on three different occasions, specifically from January 30, April 5 and May 26, 2020 via community centers and residents' committee centers.

There was an outpouring of appreciation and support such as "Clap for #SGUnited" and "Sing Together Singapore" for frontline healthcare workers, public transport workers, and those involved in other essential services.

External sector

Singapore is heavily reliant on the international supply of essential goods. Given the lockdown in Singapore and neighboring countries, as well as the shutdown of air traffic in most of the major trading countries, Singapore sought the support of countries such as Australia, Canada, Chile, New Zealand, Myanmar and Brunei to provide a continuous flow of goods and supplies amid the pandemic.[1] In addition, the Singapore government worked closely with the Chinese government to obtain relevant medical information regarding test kits and ways to fight the spread of the COVID-19 virus.

As the number of confirmed cases rose in Indonesia, Philippines, Thailand, and Malaysia, the Singapore government donated test kits, masks, ventilators, and shared information.

The Crisis among the Migrant Foreign Workers

Singapore is heavily reliant on migrant foreign workers (MFW). In 2019, lower-income foreigners such as work-permit holders and foreign

---

[1] Subhani, Ovais, Singapore working with 6 countries to maintain supply of essential goods amid coronavirus lockdowns, March 25, 2020, Straits Times, https://www.straitstimes.com/business/economy/singapore-working-with-6-other-countries-to-maintain-supply-of-essential-goods, accessed on April 27, 2020.

domestic workers comprised 70% of the 1.43 million non-residents in Singapore. This amounted to about 999,000 foreign workers, of which 293,300 were from the construction sector. While foreign domestic workers live with local families in HDB, condominiums, and landed houses, a majority of MFW working in the construction sector stay in cramped dormitories with limited access to common bathrooms and kitchens.

The outbreak of the COVID-19 virus among MFW starting in April (see Figure 2) revealed the sorry state of their living conditions and highlighted serious neglect of the welfare of this large social group. The densely populated dormitories, while economical, became the breeding ground for the virus.[2]

While the treatment of MFW needs to be improved and appropriate solutions are being discussed, prompt actions were undertaken immediately after the problem was highlighted in the government announcement of the lockdown on April 7. The public sector provided widespread testing and medical care for the affected MFW, supplied community care facilities for those who had tested positive but were not severely ill, mobilized various accommodation places around the island for the

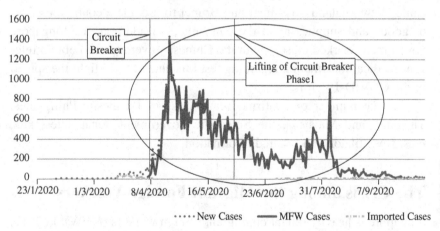

Figure 2.   New cases of COVID-19 in Singapore January–7 October 2020.

Source: The Ministry of Health, Singapore.

---

[2] As of the end of April 2020, a total of 21,000 foreign workers living in dormitories have undergone testing and more than 50% have tested positive.

healthy ones, ensured social distancing, and reassured the families of the MFW.

Also, the private sector promptly stepped forward by galvanizing financial resources and volunteers to cook, deliver, and provide psychological, emotional, and social support for the MFW. A fundraising campaign named "Migrant We Care" organized by the Migrant Worker Centre raised more than S$1.3 million among many other charitable efforts to help MFW in various ways.

As many parties played their role in a concerted and transparent manner to battle the outbreak, the confidence and trust of the MFW and the public have gradually recovered. The circuit breaker has gradually eased since June 2, 2020.

Conclusion

Singapore is a city-state that emphasizes its solidarity glue. In many parts of the world, the ongoing pandemic has revealed many deep social conflicts and fault lines beyond a public health and economic crisis. Singapore is no exception. However, it has managed to build precious social capital by rallying people from different segments of society and social strata to work together. The notion of a caring community is the core of its resilience and recipe for developing mutual trust and collective confidence.

© 2020 World Scientific Publishing Company
https://doi.org/10.1142/9789811229381_0014

Chapter 14

Ten Keys in Beating Back COVID-19 and the Associated Economic Pandemic

Shang-Jin Wei[1]

Columbia Business School, Columbia University;
Asian Bureau of Finance and Economic Research

In a Project Syndicate column that I wrote on January 27, 2020, I predicted a turning point in the spread of the novel coronavirus in China by the second or third week of February and the end of the epidemic by early May. That projection is based on a combination of the experience in ending the SARS epidemic in 2003 with aggressive government actions and the information on the life cycle of the virus. We now do see a clear turning point in China — the total number of serious and critical cases have been on a declining path since February 22, 2020, and the new case count has stayed low since mid-February.

The aggressive measures deployed by the Chinese government, including a lockdown of the city of Wuhan and surrounding areas, a mandatory extension of the holiday period throughout the country, and conversion of university courses to online offerings, have imposed tremendous

---

[1] Professor of Finance and Economics of Columbia Business School and Former Chief Economist of Asian Development Bank.

economic costs on the country in the short run. But they have bought time for other countries to ramp up the supply of the testing kits, protective clothing, and medicines (at least in principle). Unfortunately, we have since witnessed the rapid daily increases in new cases outside China in a number of countries.

When the US, Australia, and other countries first cancelled the flights between China and their countries in late January, 2020, the Chinese government took it as an affront. Now with the appearance of ineffective controls of the virus in some of these countries, the Chinese may not be eager to resume these flights any time soon.

As the virus has transitioned from an epidemic to a pandemic, it is important to take stock of the experiences and lessons thus far. This is especially important for countries not yet experiencing a widespread number of cases. And it is useful to managing the risk of future pandemics.

First, ramp up the preparation before an outbreak strikes. An outbreak will come. It is not a question of if but when. When it comes, there will be a spike in the demand for testing kits, face masks, alcohol wipes, protective clothings, hospital beds, and life support machines. Some of the countries did not use the lead time well, as reflected in a shortage of testing kits even now. Hoping that cancellation of flights is enough, or declaring that the "virus will miraculously go away" is not a good enough preparation strategy. If your country does not have a major outbreak yet, it is time to double up on your efforts and get ready.

Second, if the domestic supply of the public health material is limited, consider ramping up imports from China, Japan, and other countries of the relevant capacity. Facial masks, protective gears, and testing kits are not high-tech products and can be made in many countries. As China is the "factory of the world", appears to have had COVID-19 under control, and is eager to resume production, its factories can respond to a surge in the world demand quickly. Even many factories not currently producing the products have the knowledge and capacity to change the composition of their output to include these products. High end ECMO-like life support systems can be produced by Japan, Switzerland, and other countries. Some mid-end life-support machines can be produced and exported from

China too, including by the affiliates of multinational medical device companies in China. Also important, is that the World Bank, the IMF, and the Asian Development Bank stand ready to help, presumably including providing emergency financing for these medical imports if needed.

Third, have a workable contingency plan to ensure an adequate number of hospital beds, especially ICU beds, for infectious diseases in the event of a large-scale outbreak. Every country has to have an emergency plan specifying which hotels, university dorm, or other suitable facilities can be requisitioned and refitted in an emergency. If such a plan is infeasible or insufficient, the country needs to consider constructing new hospitals quickly. If domestic construction capacity does not allow for the same speed of construction in China (which built two brand new hospitals in Wuhan within a very short period of time), they may consider hiring Chinese companies to do the job (or companies that have a demonstrated ability to do so with speed, quality, and cost-effectiveness. In many World Bank and ADB projects involving construction of power plants, roads, and airports, Chinese companies have won the greatest number of competitive international biddings that are open to firms from all member countries. This is a testimony to the speed, quality, cost-effectiveness, and competency of Chinese companies in this area. In a public health emergency like this, when life and death is concerned and domestic capacity is limited, domestic protectionism should be set aside.

Fourth, advise the general public early, clearly, and forcefully on ways to minimize the virus spread. This includes advice on both personal hygiene (e.g., washing hands often and thoroughly) and, very importantly, social distancing (avoiding crowds and unnecessary gatherings, disinfecting doorknobs and bus/train seats). Two types of governments failed in this regard in the initial phase of the pandemic. Authoritarian governments may suppress the epidemic information to maintain their public "image" before the problem gets out of their control, and anti-science governments may downplay the seriousness of the problems for fear of a negative impact on stock prices and election outcomes. Fortunately, since the World Health Organization has already declared COVID-19 a pandemic, the risk of active suppression of the seriousness of the problem has subsided. However, not every government has succeeded in conveying clear and trustworthy advice to the public, consistent with the best available medical knowledge. A good model to emulate is Singapore, where the health officials and even the Prime Minister has delivered a series of informative and medically accurate information to the public. While Singapore had some early count of infection cases and a small second wave, it has been broadly successful in limiting community spread in spite of a high level of inter-connectedness in both economic and people ties with Mainland China. Its wise and trusted advice from the government has played an important role.

Fifth, take early and decisive actions to enforce social distancing as soon as there are signs of an outbreak. As Tomas Pueyo points out, because the official case count records people who have had symptoms and sought medical assistance a few days after the onset of infection, they are a delayed account of what is going on in the society. There is generally a gap on any given day between the true count of new infection cases and the officially recorded new cases. Importantly, the systematic bias changes signs in two stages. In general, in the early stage, the true count tends to be substantially higher than the officially recorded case count. In the second stage, after the containment becomes successful, the turning point in the true count also tends to occur a few days ahead of the turning point in the official case count. Based on this insight, Pueyo calculates that as soon as the lockdown in Wuhan and the mandatory social distancing started in the rest of the China, the downward trend in the "true case count" followed almost immediately afterwards. This suggests that aggressive social distancing is both effective in China and likely necessary in any country that wants to see a relatively quick turnaround in the spread of the disease.

Sixth, emergency assistance to workers, firms, and financial firms need to be put in place quickly. While aggressive social distancing is important in turning around the pandemic, it will exert strong negative impact on the overall economy in the short turn, and potentially a big negative impact in some sectors even in the medium run. The closure of factories and schools and cancellation of product exhibits and work conferences are a negative shock to the supply, and the impact of the shock can be transmitted via supply chains to downstream sectors around the world, including to countries not currently experiencing a major virus outbreak. In addition, the pandemic is also causing a contraction of income and demand, whose impact can transmit via supply chains to upstream sectors around the world, again including to countries not yet experiencing any major virus outbreak. During this period, wages, utilities, bank loans, and other expenses need to be paid. Many business firms have a limited cash reserve, perhaps not enough to cover expenses for more than three to six months. This is especially true for micro, small, and medium enterprises. Moreover, the decline in business and the rise in uncertainty can cause households and companies to cut down spending, even in the absence of store closures and quarantine requirements. This means that there could be a downward spiral (or self-fulfilling expectation) in the contraction in demand for each other's products and services. This logic means that governments have to roll out an emergency economic assistance program, including temporary suspension of tax and interest payments, financial assistance and guaranteed health benefits to workers who have to stay at home due to the virus, financial assistance to banks to forestall large-scale financial sector failure, and reduction or elimination of import duties for medical supplies and protective garments.

Seventh, make the best or better usage of the digital age. Much of offline retail shopping can be replaced by online shopping but this requires the country to have a broad reach of internet, widespread acceptance of digital payment by merchants and households, and an efficient and inexpensive delivery system. China is fortunate to possess all three attributes. A suspension of the delivery service in the early phase of the epidemic control has now been relaxed. Much of the remnants of resistance to digital payment (typically via Alipay or WeChat pay), mostly by elderly, has given away to near complete acceptance of digital payment out of necessity. Countries that are relatively deficient in these areas can find ways to ramp up the capacity. If there is a shortage of domestic talent or capacity, there are quite a few international companies in digital payment and online retailing that can come to the country expeditiously if the policy environment is open and conducive. If not, this is the time to consider emergency service sector reforms in all areas that can help to advance public health objectives.

Eighth, turn the increased usage of internet into a more permanent enhancement of long-run economic growth potential. Once a large proportion of student learning and worker training go online, there can be an acceleration in the pace of human capital accumulation. The world does not need 10,000 physics, mathematics, or economics professors teaching the basics of these subjects. Instead, all students can learn from perhaps the top 10 professors globally as they expound on their knowledge and ideas. This will not only reduce the access gap to the best teachers between the most elite and least privileged schools, but will also free up local resources to provide better targeted questions-and-answer sessions or increase the variety of course offerings. This technological possibility existed before the coronavirus. But old habits die hard and people and institutions naturally find it difficult to change since change involves some physical or mental switching costs. The experimentation with massive online learning that is necessitated by the pandemic control could be the necessary nudge to produce a permanent change of habit. Hopefully, more governments and communities will see the potential of the digital economy, the potential for the students and workers training to learn from the global best, and make policy changes and corresponding investment, so as to better utilize this potential.

Ninth, an internationally coordinated economic stimulus program will be more effective in reducing global recessionary pressure than isolated actions of individual countries. This is especially true for fiscal stimulus. When a country pursues fiscal expansion on its own, such as a payroll tax cut or a temporary financial assistance to households in need, the increase domestic demand may "leak" to foreign producers in the form of an appreciation of the domestic currency and higher imports of foreign products. The leakage is especially big for small and medium-sized countries that have a relatively high ratio of import/GDP ratio. This may disincentivize the countries from pursuing enough fiscal stimulus. An international coordination of simultaneous fiscal expansion can solve this problem. When all countries raise their total demand, the exchange rates do not need to move or at least do not move as much as when each country acts alone. The increase in the world demand will be good for all countries. The required coordination goes beyond the G-7 countries, and will require stronger cooperation at the G-20 level, or under the auspices of the IMF or the World Bank.

Tenth, reducing tariffs and non-tariff trade barriers can also help to fight a pandemic-induced recession. As the US Federal Reserve and the European Central Bank have already cut their policy interest rates to nearly zero, there is a limit to how much more the central banks can do to stimulate the economy. Yet, many countries still maintain various trade barriers that both raise the costs of production and reduce the real incomes of their households. While the risk of an economic recession often tempts countries to raise trade barriers, the exact opposite is needed to boost global output and employment. Similar to the logic underlying a coordinated fiscal expansion, coordinated trade liberalization has a better chance of overcoming domestic protectionist resistance as each country's policy "concession" to foreign firms is met with improved access for their own firms to foreign markets. The WTO and the G-20 need to step up their leadership in this area and act fast. One natural question is whether the United States, a traditional promoter of trade liberalization but an instigator of unilateral trade wars of the last three years, will join this effort. There are reasons to be hopeful: when the US initiated the trade wars three years ago, the negative effect was hiding behind an economy over-stimulated by a massive tax cut. Now that the sugar high from the tax cut is almost gone and the US faces the risk of a recession, perhaps the US administration's calculation would be different and it will be more open to a coordinated trade liberalization, especially if it can be combined with reforms at the WTO that it seeks.

The coronavirus pandemic is moving the world towards a rare and serious disaster, but it is also offering a rare chance for the world community to undertake a number of policy changes to not only address the short-term public health challenge but also boost long-term growth potential. While not all interesting sayings attributed to the Chinese actually originate from Chinese, it is true that the Chinese expression for "crisis" consists of a word for "danger" and another one for "opportunity." Let us seize the moment and not waste the crisis.

© 2020 World Scientific Publishing Company
https://doi.org/10.1142/9789811229381_0015

Chapter 15

Heuristics in Policymaking: It's Time to Figure Out What Drives Policy Uncertainty

Xiao Ji, Mengyu Wang and Hong Zhang

PBC School of Finance, Tsinghua University

Abstract

Policymaking under the pandemic pressure could be subject to cognitive heuristics, allowing the resulting policy uncertainty to influence the market negatively.

Researches in economics and finance have long recognized the importance of policy uncertainty. However, most studies take policy uncertainty as a given while focusing on its real or financial influences. The few studies exploring the economic sources of policy uncertainty often attribute it to some sort of external uncertainty faced by the government in making policies.[1]

---

[1] Baker *et al.* (2014), for instance, suggest that the increasing trend in the Economic Policy Uncertainty index (Baker, Bloom and Davis 2016) could reflect enhanced government activities and heated political polarization in the US. In Pástor and Veronesi (2012, 2013), policy uncertainty arises due to the stochastic political costs of different potential policies, for which both the government and companies need to learn. In the literature on

The coronavirus pandemic of 2020 tells a different story. Its influence on the stock market is unpreceded (Baker *et al.* 2020, Fetzer *et al.* 2020). Conditioning on the same uncertainty of the pandemic, however, governments across the world formulate and announce different policies. The drastically different real and financial impacts of such policies remind us that policy uncertainty could directly originate from the decision process of policymakers. It is time to figure out what drives policy uncertainty and how to optimize policymaking under crisis.

A Case Study of Italy and Taiwan

A case study on pandemic-related policymaking provides some hints. We take all official pandemic announcements (i.e., the pandemic "policies") from the government web of a list of countries/regions. We then apply a linguistic analysis of Loughran and McDonald (2011) in creating an "uncertainty sentiment score" for government-released polices — our measure of *policy uncertainty* — with a high score indicating a high frequency of using uncertain words in announcing policies. In Figure 1, we plot the policy uncertainty score for Taiwan and Italy. "Day one" in the graph indicates the first date for the number of coronavirus cases to hit 20 in each place.

From the figure, we can observe several interesting features. First, the frequency of government announcements differs drastically. The policy announcements of Taiwan occur at a daily frequency across the pandemic period, whereas those from Italy are more sporadic. Second, the variance of policy uncertainty in Taiwan is relatively small, whereas the uncertainty can change drastically from one policy to another for Italy. Among the other countries, Singapore also has a relatively small range of policy uncertainty. Finally, although the expansion of coronavirus cases is at a much slower pace in Taiwan, the average level of uncertainty embedded in its pandemic policies is not visibly smaller.

Jointly, Taiwan's policymaking seems to follow a precautionary principle (e.g., Arrow and Fisher 1974), whereas Italy processes policies

---

environmental policies, policy uncertainty is often directly linked to the uncertainty nature of environmental damages and the real resource costs of mitigating such damages.

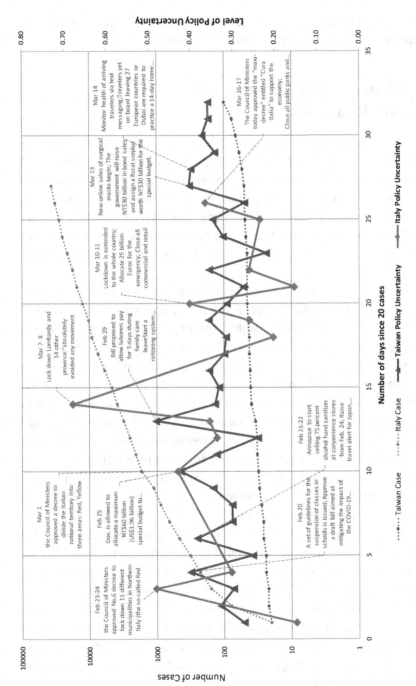

Figure 1. Policy uncertainly (Italy versus Taiwan).

differently. What could explain such a deviation? Could policy uncertainty of different origins impact the market differently?

Heuristics in Policymaking and Market Responses

It is well-known that, when people need to make judgments and decisions quickly, they often resort to shortcuts, or "heuristics" (e.g., Simon 1956, Kahneman *et al.* 1982). Although it is widely believed that heuristics are the choices of people with limited cognitive or information resources and that policymaking should be rational, optimal, and precautious, the pandemic has trapped policymakers in an urgent situation to move fast. Hence the question: Could policymakers resort to heuristics in making policies in this case?

Drawing from our other ongoing research on environmental policy uncertainty, we conjecture that a relevant economic ground could be extrapolative expectations. Roughly speaking, policymaking subject to this type of heuristics may overuse short-term information and result in myopic policies embedding big swings of policy uncertainty. For instance, the February 22, 2020 policy announcement by the Italian government (Italy's "Day 1" in the plot) contains much less uncertainty than the comparable policy announcement of Taiwan on its Day 1. But the next major policy announcement by the Italian government on February 24, 2020 witnessed a surge in uncertainty score, followed by a falling uncertainty again on the next date. This pattern is consistent with the heuristics of initially underestimating the influence of pandemic and subsequently extrapolating its short-term expansion.

Compared to precautionary policymaking, heuristics-based policy uncertainty may have more unintended consequences in the real economy. Conditioning on the same level of uncertainty, for instance, the latter type may attract more market volatility or negative sentiment. Table 1 below is a simple data analysis, in which we pool the government announcements of the US, UK, Singapore, Japan, Taiwan, and Italy, and regress market responses (in terms of future volatility and return) on policy uncertainty. We use lagged market responses to control for the time-invariant characteristics of each market.

Table 1. Data analysis of market responses to government announcements.

Y = market response	Market Volatility (t + 1: t + 5)			Market Return (t + 1: t + 5)			Market Return (t + 1)		
	Model 1	Model 2	Model 3	Model 4	Model 5	Model 6	Model 7	Model 8	Model 9
Intercept	−1.170*	−0.929	−1.188*	−0.017	−0.023	−0.025	−0.013*	−0.014**	−0.014**
	(−1.759)	(−1.401)	(−1.776)	(−0.981)	(−1.288)	(−1.468)	(−1.825)	(−1.990)	(−2.005)
Policy Uncertainty (t)	6.136***	7.030***	6.269***	−0.056	−0.067	−0.021	0.002	−0.003	0.010
	(2.855)	(3.268)	(2.872)	(−1.028)	(−1.236)	(−0.385)	(0.075)	(−0.130)	(0.410)
Policy Uncertainty of Taiwan		−3.970**			0.076*			0.028*	
		(−2.342)			(1.916)			(1.672)	
Policy Uncertainty of Italy			−0.988			−0.200***			−0.061**
			(−0.386)			(−3.085)			(−2.169)
Lagged Y (t − 4: t)	0.990***	0.918***	0.991***	0.348**	0.271	0.260	−0.241***	−0.251***	−0.279***
	(14.377)	(12.319)	(14.340)	(2.018)	(1.545)	(1.533)	(−2.828)	(−2.947)	(−3.239)
R-Square	0.602	0.616	0.602	0.035	0.062	0.040	0.050	0.067	0.078
Observations	151	151	151	134	134	134	156	156	156

Note: Statistical significance at the 1%, 5%, and 10% levels is denoted by ***, **, and *, respectively.

From Model 1, we can see that market volatility is positively related to policy uncertainty for the pool of countries. While this result is not surprising, an interesting observation is that, as Model 2 suggests, the policy uncertainty of Taiwan has a much smaller influence on volatility than other countries. Italy exhibits no difference in terms of market volatility.

Models 4 to 6 tell a different influence of policy uncertainty of Taiwan and Italy in terms of the market return. While policy uncertainty on average is unrelated to market returns, the Italy Policy Uncertainty unambiguously gives rise to negative market sentiment.

In brief, the precautionary policymaking of Taiwan does not lead to more volatile and negative market response, whereas the arguable influence of heuristics on Italy's policymaking induces the market to respond negatively to policy uncertainty.

Policymaking at WHO

The influence of heuristics on policy uncertainty is not limited to governments. Large international organizations, such as the World Health Organization (WHO), may also be potentially subject to decision heuristics. To examine this possibility, we apply the same linguistic analysis to WHO. We then compare the policy uncertainty of WHO to that of Taiwan.

Figure 2 plots the policy uncertainty of WHO and Taiwan on calendar dates. A noticeable observation in early January 2020, is that the dynamics of Taiwan's policy uncertainty lead that of WHO, suggesting that Taiwan had responded very fast to the early-stage development of the pandemic. Despite this initial similarity, the WHO policy announcements exhibit more considerable variations in policy uncertainty than Taiwan. For instance, WHO's policy uncertainty had dropped to very low around January 28 and then bounced around between a much broader range of policy uncertainty in the following days. These properties suggest that WHO is perhaps similar to Italy and could be vulnerable to heuristics in policymaking.

Concluding Remarks

Although evidence on the impact of heuristics in decision-making is overwhelming, how heuristics affect the economy through policymaking

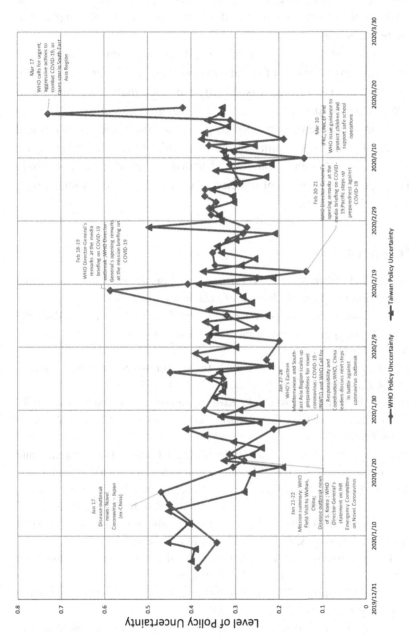

Figure 2. Policy uncertainty of WHO in calender dates.

remains largely unexplored. During the pandemic, heuristics may become a fundamental economic source to influence policymaking and to give rise to policy uncertainty.

Of course, our analysis is anecdotal and very preliminary. There could be alternative explanations of the above observations. Baker *et al.* (2020), for instance, discuss several reasons why the stock market has responded so strongly to the pandemic since late February 2020 in the US. More research, in this regard, is needed to pin down the potential origin and influence of policy uncertainty in the pandemic. In a broader sense, we believe that a better understanding of heuristics in policymaking could help explain the dispersion of policies as well as related economic developments around the world.

References

Arrow, K.J. and Fisher, A.C., 1974. Environmental preservation, uncertainty, and irreversibility. *Quarterly Journal of Economics,* 88, 312–319.

Baker, S.R., Bloom, N., Canes-Wrone, B., Davis, S.J. and Rodden, J., 2014. Why has US policy uncertainty risen since 1960? *American Economic Review,* 104(5), 56–60.

Baker, S.R., Bloom, N. and Davis, S.J., 2016. Measuring economic policy uncertainty. *Quarterly Journal of Economics,* 131(4), 1593–1636.

Baker, S.R., Bloom, N., Davis, S.J., Kost, K., Sammon, M. and Viratyosin, T., 2020. The unprecedented stock market reaction to COVID-19. *The Review of Asset Pricing Studies.*

Fetzer, T., Hensel, L., Hermle, J. and Roth, C., 2020. Coronavirus perceptions and economic anxiety. *Review of Economics and Statistics,* 1–36.

Kahneman, D., Slovic, S.P., Slovic, P. and Tversky, A. eds., 1982. *Judgment under Uncertainty: Heuristics and Biases.* Cambridge: Cambridge University Press.

Loughran, T. and McDonald, B., 2011. When is a liability not a liability? Textual analysis, dictionaries, and 10-Ks. *Journal of Finance,* 66(1), 35–65.

Pástor, Ľ. and Veronesi, P., 2012. Uncertainty about government policy and stock prices. *Journal of Finance,* 67(4), 1219–1264.

Pástor, Ľ. and Veronesi, P., 2013. Political uncertainty and risk premia. *Journal of Financial Economics,* 110(3), 520–545.

Simon, H.A., 1956. Rational choice and the structure of the environment. *Psychological Review,* 63(2), 129.

© 2020 World Scientific Publishing Company
https://doi.org/10.1142/9789811229381_0016

Chapter 16

What Comes to Mind: Some Reflections on COVID-19

Yueran Ma

Booth School of Business, University of Chicago

Do you remember New Year's Eve of 2020? When you saw the splendid fireworks at midnight and made your New Year's wishes, could you have imagined what would happen in the next few months?

If you live in China, do you remember the first time you heard about some virus affecting Wuhan? When you skimmed through the news at the end of a long day, could you have imagined that this small piece of information would change the path of the entire country, and subsequently, the entire world?

If you live in Europe, do you remember the time when you heard about the coronavirus affecting several towns near Milan? When you pictured the Italian villages in your head, could you have imagined the life and death choices Italy had to face after two short weeks?

If you live in the US, do you remember the week when you heard about the coronavirus outbreak in a Seattle nursing home and suspected community transmission in California? When you thought about friends and family living in Seattle and California, could you have imagined that there would be more than 100,000 reported cases across the country in less than a month, and more than one million reported cases in two months?

In retrospect, it may seem that everything all happened too quickly. It may seem that there were so many moments when the catastrophe could have been stopped. Why did we fail to seize those moments and turn the tide?

The situation is still evolving, so statements and views formed at this point may need to be recalibrated with the passage of time and the accumulation of new evidence. Commentaries from researchers in many fields have also been emerging at a rapid speed, and many important points have already been made. I will focus my reflections on three areas: belief formation, individual responses, and societal responses. The common theme throughout the discussion is that people's perceptions and decisions can be significantly influenced by how easily a scenario or an idea can come to mind, which may pose substantial challenges for addressing epidemics where the situation is unfamiliar, rapidly changing, and requires an extensive degree of individual cooperation.

Belief Formation: Novelty, Invisibility, and Exponential Growth

For an epidemic, awareness is essential, but raising awareness can be challenging.

One lesson from research in behavioral economics and psychology is that people often have a difficult time imagining a world that is significantly different from what they see at the moment. Memory is by association, and recall is cued by the current context. Scenarios that are very different from the current situation are less available in our minds. This is a usual suspect for why we see rather pervasive over-extrapolation of recent trends in financial markets and in other domains. This is also a plausible suspect for why we may neglect tail risks and black swans.

The problem is worse in the COVID-19 context because a large-scale epidemic is unfamiliar, the virus is invisible (and symptoms take a long time to appear or may not appear), and the infections grow exponentially. With this combination, it is extra difficult for people to realize that although the current situation may seem okay, the world can be completely different in a week or two. We cannot visibly see the presence and damage of the epidemic until it is too late.

The limitations we may have for envisioning a world turned upside down is a fundamental issue for raising awareness, especially at the early and critical stage of the epidemic. It can be difficult to convince people of the danger and scope of the epidemic when the threat is invisible and unfamiliar, yet destined to grow exponentially. As a result, the same pattern seems to repeat itself in many part of the world — the threat is underestimated or ignored by individuals and governments when things appear normal, and only recognized when it is too late.

Since early February, prominent epidemiologists have warned that an epidemic in the US and a global pandemic are likely. When this possibility was brought up in conversations at the time, it was often dismissed. In late February, when rumors — followed by news — came out that community transmission was present in the US, there was an interesting sharp contrast between the perception among the Chinese community and the perception among the general public in the US. For the Chinese group, the memory of SARS and the suffering of Wuhan unfolded in front of people's eyes, and many became very nervous about the prospects of the US. Preparing hand sanitizers, Clorox wipes, masks, gloves, food (and some even suggested various forms of oxygen machines) became a first-order issue. Meanwhile, life went on as usual for most Americans. Experience effects have long been recognized in economics research, and past experiences shape the availability of different types of memories. With limited experiences of major fast-moving epidemics for nearly a century, it is natural that the American population was not highly alarmed for some period of time. In many cities, marathons, parties, and St. Patrick's Day celebrations persisted into mid-March. Even after cities and states rolled out stay-at-home orders, many places continued to see crowds forming in public spaces, which highlights the challenges of raising awareness and helping people recognize the severity of the problem.

Individual Responses: Internalizing Externalities

Another key feature of epidemic control is that it typically requires an extensive amount of individual cooperation, and each person's behavior can have substantial externalities. With the long incubation period as well as asymptomatic transmission, individuals who socialize in crowded spaces can unknowingly spread COVID-19 to a very large group of people. Especially in societies that respect individual freedom and feel uneasy about imposing strict lockdowns, the implementation of social distancing relies heavily on individuals' decisions.

What we have seen in the US since March seems to indicate that self-enforcement of social distancing is not easy. We may feel confident that we will not fall ill or die. It is much less salient in mind that even if we do not get critically ill, we may be responsible for transmitting the virus to others, and then may be further responsible for crowding the medical system. When you have a beer with a friend, the fact that someone you don't know several steps down the social interaction chain may be an 80-year-old grandfather with cancer does not typically come to mind. The fact that the grandpa, if ill and hospitalized, may require intensive care for a long period of time or may die is even harder to register. What captures your attention is much more likely the beer, the conversation, and the immediate surroundings.

From packed beaches to crowds of protesters, in the past few months there are many reminders that individual behavior may not place significant weights on externalities. Even if people perceive the risks to be low for themselves, their actions could create additional risks for family members, neighbors, and others they come into contact with (e.g., workers at grocery stores and gas stations), which may not be taken into account. In some protests, medical professionals confronted the protesters and asked them to consider the risks they create for doctors and nurses, to limited success. Given that textbooks are already filled with examples of the challenges in dealing with externalities, this issue perhaps should not come as a surprise. But personal experiences tend to be particularly vivid, and I have certainly come to internalize this classic lesson more than before.

Societal Responses: Precautions, Priorities, and Efficiency

The nature of the epidemic tends to require a substantial amount of social and governmental intervention, for a long list of reasons. First, with all the challenges of self-enforcing social distancing, such as limited awareness and extensive externalities, governments often need to step in to impose and enforce strict requirements on social activities. Second, to decrease infections, ideally one wants to identify and separate individuals who are sick versus healthy. This process requires testing, contact tracing, and quarantines, which also need government resources and coordination. Third, if hospitals become overwhelmed and experience serious shortages of medical equipment and personnel, governments need to provide emergency funding and supplies. Finally, there are numerous types of economic impact from social distancing (e.g., layoffs and unemployment, financial distress of households and firms, strains on the financial system) that may require government response.

There is sometimes a theme in political discussions that confronting the epidemic has a rather strict conflict with maintaining economic activities. Nonetheless, there are measures that may decrease infections with relatively limited economic costs. Some of these measures are familiar, such as avoiding handshakes and washing hands frequently, which were the focus of the initial public communication in the US. Other measures may be less familiar, socially and culturally. For example, wearing masks can be helpful. If anything, it prevents people from using hands to touch the face and the mouth. If more workers are equipped with masks and gloves that help to limit transmission, more economic activities can be sustained. For another example, turning hotels into quarantine housing for patients with mild cases could be helpful. Home quarantine comes with the problem that family members may get infected, and transmission within households appears to account for a substantial fraction of known cases.

Many of these measures, to a smaller or larger extent, break with the familiar lifestyles people have. Governments are inevitably slow to adopt measures that are unfamiliar based on existing lifestyles and mindsets. In East Asia where using masks is commonplace in part because of air pollution issues, requiring individuals to wear masks in public spaces is relatively straightforward. In the US where masks are unfamiliar and perhaps commonly associated with sickness, the government spent months campaigning for wearing them among the general population. In East Asia where privacy concerns are weaker and social compliance is stronger, contact tracing and centralized quarantines are easier to roll out. In the US where privacy notions are strong and individual freedom is essential, pushing for contact tracing and central quarantine could be tricky. The main alternative to such targeted separation strategies is blanket separation strategies like region-wide or country-wide stay-at-home requirements or lockdowns, which tend to come at higher economic costs.

In addition, in many parts of the world, governments have struggled to set priorities straight, in response to the epidemic. In the US, it is not uncommon to come across political resistance against social distancing and epidemic control. Nonetheless, early and effective epidemic control is likely to be helpful, rather than detrimental, to the economy. Exemplar countries like South Korea have been able to do so, in which case new infections fell back to close to zero reasonably quickly and economic disruptions have been relatively limited. In other parts of the world, we see that the longer the epidemic drags on and the larger it becomes, the harder it is for economic activities to get back to normal. In some cases, there seems to be no clear end in sight. The human costs are also becoming tragically high, which could be harmful for social stability and cohesiveness.

The idea that epidemic control is important, and the usual priority of economic growth may be achieved indirectly, is not necessarily obvious or appealing to some decision-makers. When one is preoccupied with economic statistics in the near term, and has limited capacity to think beyond the next month or two, the order of priorities may end up being misplaced. It is also not uncommon that immediate, partial equilibrium results are easier for people to think about than overall, general equilibrium impact. With all these challenges, some countries have seen painful struggles with societal priorities that tend to result in a lack of intervention in the early stage and rushing too quickly to reopen in the later stage.

At the moment, with the combination of inadequate initial responses, a prolonged lack of testing and contact tracing, and the infeasibility of strict lockdowns and quarantines, the prospect of eliminating new infections appears increasing unlikely in the US. The society then faces the challenging task of living with COVID-19 until there is a vaccine or widespread immunity. Many things we took for granted may not be possible for a long time. Adapting to this brave new world and coping with unfamiliar situations could be a constant theme in the foreseeable future.

Lessons and Memories

The pandemic of COVID-19 presents a large set of challenges. Small things that we do in the near term may have large and persistent impact in the long term. The number of infections can grow exponentially. The social and political consequences could also grow exponentially. The lives of tens of thousands of individuals, the viability of "life as we know it," the trust in governments, and the promise of economic prosperity are all at stake. Effective epidemic control, however, tends to require us to grapple with many things that we are not familiar with and things that do not come to mind easily. Raising awareness, internalizing externalities, utilizing precautionary measures, and setting priorities straight all appear challenging at times, as we slowly and imperfectly transition into the new reality.

Even if many things could go wrong this time, one might still hope that we may at least learn some general lessons and form some collective memories that will guide us in unprecedented situations in the future. However, there is the risk that some lessons and associations people form from this experience may not be socially beneficial, such as connecting the epidemic with certain ethnicities. If a vaccine is on the horizon in the next year or two, the short-term turmoil will perhaps eventually pass, but the long-term impact is too early to predict. Ten or twenty years from now, when people encounter the term COVID-19, what will come to mind?

Part IV

Implications on International Credit and Trade

© 2020 World Scientific Publishing Company
https://doi.org/10.1142/9789811229381_0017

Chapter 17

The COVID-19 Pandemic Exposes Asian Banks' Vulnerability to US Dollar Funding[1]

Cyn-Young Park and Peter Rosenkranz

Asian Development Bank

The COVID-19 pandemic has been unraveling global financial markets and testing Asia's financial resilience at a time that Asian and global economic activity have slowed due to prolonged trade uncertainties. While it began as a health crisis, this pandemic could turn into an economic and financial crisis if not swiftly contained. Across the region, stock markets have crashed, currencies have tumbled, and short-term capital has taken flight, underscoring fragile market sentiments. Amid flight to safety, the demand for the US dollar has soared. While multiple factors (primarily driven by fear of a precipitous economic slowdown) are behind the surge in demand, it is a global rush to unwind carry trades that drove a rise in dollar funding costs in the interbank and foreign exchange swap markets (Figure 1).

---

[1]The authors thank Mara Claire Tayag, Ana Kristel Lapid and Monica Melchor for their excellent research assistance.

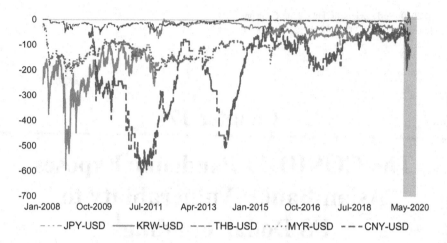

Figure 1.   Cross-currency basis swap (basis points), January 1, 2008–May 8, 2020.

CNY = Chinese yuan, JPY = Japanese yen, KRW = Korean won, MYR = Malaysian ringgit, THB = Thai baht, USD = US dollar.

Note: Data as of 8 May 2020. 3-month cross-currency basis swap for JPY-USD, MYR-USD and CNY-USD; 6-month for THB-USD; and 3-month versus 6-month for KRW-USD.

Source: Bloomberg (accessed 8 May 2020).

The global reliance on short-term dollar funding proved to be the Achilles' heel of the international monetary and financial system more than a decade ago and it still is. The US dollar is the dominant currency for international trade and financial transactions. With continuously growing international business and financial activities, non-US banks with active overseas operations (i.e., non-US global banks) have become major intermediaries of US dollar-denominated cross-border lending and international debt issuance. Given their limited access to a stable dollar deposit base, non-US global banks tend to rely more on short-term and potentially volatile wholesale funding for their dollar liquidity needs than US global banks.

Prior to the global financial crisis (GFC) of 2008, European banks had increased their dollar-denominated lending to emerging market economies sharply. The Bank for International Settlements (BIS) reports that European banks held cross-border assets denominated in US dollar reaching more than $8 trillion in early 2008, which was ten times more than US banks' assets denominated in European currencies.[2] They tapped short-term money markets for their dollar financing needs, while their emerging market assets were not short-term. When Lehman's bankruptcy hit the money markets, European banks rushed to foreign exchange swap markets to turn their euro funding to US dollar funding through the use of derivatives. The acute asymmetry in the foreign exchange swap markets in favor of the US dollar further exacerbated the increase in dollar funding costs. The subsequent massive deleveraging of European banks propagated financial stress from distressed lenders to emerging market borrowers.

Fast forward to today, the US dollar continues to be the currency of choice for cross-border banking activity. Since the GFC, non-US global banks have continued to expand their US dollar-denominated credits to governments and corporate borrowers around the world. In particular, an extended period of very low interest rates in advanced economies has reignited international lending in US dollar to emerging market borrowers. Cross-border banking activities of non-US banks have steadily increased over the past decade, with their dollar assets surpassing the pre-GFC peak of $9.4 trillion in 2008 Q1 to reach $11.6 trillion in 2019 Q3.[3]

The same mechanism whereby non-US global banks raise dollar funding for cross-border lending remains a source of vulnerability for the global financial system, but major players have changed. First, severely hit by the GFC and the eurozone debt crisis, European banks have reduced their cross-border dollar assets. Second, non-European, non-US banks — particularly in Australia, Canada, Japan, and Singapore — came to pick up the slack left by European banks. Finally, as post-GFC financial regulatory reforms have limited excessive risk-taking and leverage of global banks, non-bank creditors have emerged to assume a greater share of dollar-denominated debt securities issued by emerging market governments and corporate borrowers. While these structural changes, combined

---

[2]Baba, N., R. McCauley and S. Ramaswamy. 2009. "US dollar money market funds and non-US banks". *BIS Quarterly Review.* https://www.bis.org/publ/qtrpdf/r_qt0903g.pdf.

[3]International Monetary Fund. 2019. *Global Financial Stability Report: Lower for Longer.* https://www.imf.org/~/media/Files/Publications/GFSR/2019/October/English/ch5.ashx?la=en.

with more stringent regulations, have improved the balance sheet resilience of global banks in general, they have had unintended effects on dollar funding markets and therefore vulnerabilities of emerging Asian economies, in particular.

Non-US global banks rely more on foreign exchange swap markets for dollar funding, while prevailing currency and maturity mismatches facing them have been largely unresolved. The BIS estimated that foreign exchange swap contracts involving US dollar reached around $53 trillion at end-June 2019, more than double the amount from end 2009.[4]

Asian banks have substantially increased international activities over the past two decades, with a high share of about 80% denominated in foreign currency (primarily in US dollar) as of 2019 Q3. Cross-border banking operations increased on both the claims and liabilities sides of Asian banks (Figure 2). Banks in high income Asian economies have increased their dollar-denominated lending, while banks in emerging Asian economies have borrowed in US dollars. This implies the substantial increase in underlying dollar funding needs for Asian banks through foreign exchange swap markets.

Asian banks have been also increasingly engaged with non-bank counterparts in cross-border banking activities, with 58% of Asian banks' claims and 40% of their liabilities being on non-banks as of 2019 Q3 (Figure 3). While the amount of cross-border activities vis-à-vis foreign banks has remained largely stable in recent years, activities with non-banks have ballooned. This in turn exposes vulnerabilities of Asian banks as large global non-bank investors may pull out capital from emerging market economies during financial turbulence.

A sudden squeeze in dollar funding liquidity, combined with unwinding of carry trades by non-US global banks, can quickly spill over to emerging market borrowers. As some high-income Asian economies have now substituted European banks in credit expansion in Asia, they will be forced to curtail their lending to emerging Asian economies, which will amplify financial shocks to the region's economies. Increased participation of Asian non-bank players in international lending together with their

---

[4]Avdjiev, S., E. Eren and P. McGuire. 2020. *BIS Bulletin* 1. https://www.bis.org/publ/bis-bull01.pdf.

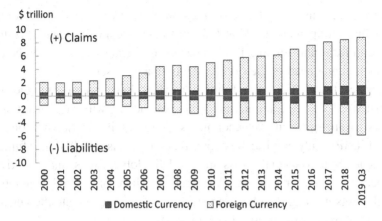

Figure 2.   Gross cross-border bank claims and liabilities, domestic and foreign currency, Asia.

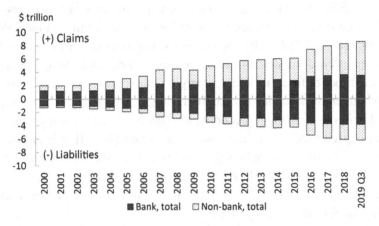

Figure 3.   Gross cross-border bank claims and liabilities, bank and non-bank sector, Asia.

Notes: Asia and the Pacific includes Australia; the People's Republic of China; Hong Kong, China; Indonesia; India; Japan; the Republic of Korea; Malaysia; the Philippines; Singapore; and Taipei,China. Data for the People's Republic of China beginning 2015, Indonesia beginning 2010, India beginning 2001, Malaysia 2007, the Philippines beginning 2016, and the Republic of Korea beginning 2005. For total claims, domestic currency for Hong Kong, China (2000-2012); and Malaysia were deduced by subtracting foreign currency claims from total claims. For total liabilities, domestic currency for Hong Kong, China (2000-2012); Malaysia; and Singapore were deduced by subtracting foreign currency liabilities from total liabilities.

Source: BIS Locational Banking Statistics (accessed March 26, 2020) for reporting economies in Asia and the Pacific.

currency hedging activities also adds an extra layer of stress on foreign exchange swap markets. Non-US corporate and institutional investors' demand for dollar funding has increased significantly and so has the currency hedging need of their dollar-denominated assets.

Since the GFC, dollar funding markets have become increasingly sensitive to macroeconomic and financial shocks, with significant spillovers to emerging market economies. A recent International Monetary Fund (IMF) study empirically shows that an increase in US dollar funding costs leads to financial stress in non-US global banks and negatively affects cross-border lending.[5] The growing share of US dollar assets to total assets in the global banking systems seem to aggravate the negative effects of extenuating dollar funding markets.

Overall, Asia's banking systems have made great improvements in their balance sheet health and financial resilience since the sweeping reforms following the Asian financial crisis more than two decades ago and the GFC more than a decade ago. However, they remain vulnerable to disruptions in global dollar funding markets given the large expansion of their cross-border activities and exposures to currency hedging positions. During times of financial stress, emerging market borrowers are also typically vulnerable to capital flow and exchange rate volatility. A depreciating local currency against the US dollar also decreases an economy's balance sheet capacity, due to an increase in the value of (dollar-denominated) liabilities relative to the asset side, resulting in a further tightening of local financial conditions. While some disparities are observed at the country level, Asian economies' foreign currency liabilities in aggregate exceed their total foreign currency claims.

At this stage, one cannot discount the possibility of another financial crash, nor of some countries experiencing debt crises. As the prolonged COVID-19 pandemic combined with continued social distancing and mobility restrictions pushes the global economy into a recession, there is a risk of many economies entering a vicious cycle, starting from defaults and bankruptcies in the private sector, leading to a credit crunch or even a

---

[5] International Monetary Fund. 2019. *Global Financial Stability Report: Lower for Longer*. https://www.imf.org/~/media/Files/Publications/GFSR/2019/October/English/ch5.ashx?la=en.

financial crisis. This, in turn, would exacerbate Asia's vulnerability to US dollar funding, amplifying negative spillovers to financial markets. However, given Asia's strong underlying economic fundamentals, timely, appropriate policies can help prevent a prolonged recession and steer a swift economic recovery. It is therefore very important that regional policymakers take bold action to strengthen crisis preparedness and mitigate the negative impacts through better management of global and regional financial safety net arrangements.

First, the highest policy priority should be to sustain market confidence and ensure adequate liquidity. Maintaining macrofinancial policies that are supportive of the economy and markets is key, while ensuring that emergency monetary and fiscal support measures are deemed sustainable. Asian central banks have already opted to inject emergency liquidity to the markets using conventional and unconventional measures, while many governments have been rolling out fiscal stimulus packages including tax relief, demand subsidies, and social security, as well as loans and loan guarantees for badly affected businesses. Such containment efforts and large-scale stimulus packages can help significantly decrease the probability of a global recession.

Second, the bilateral currency swap lines extended by the US Federal Reserve (Fed) helped arrest market panic at a time of extreme financial volatility in March 2020. The Fed has standing swap lines with the Bank of Canada, the Bank of England, the Bank of Japan, the European Central Bank, and the Swiss National Bank. On March 19, 2020, it announced the establishment of temporary dollar liquidity swap lines with 9 additional central banks, including Australia, Rep. of Korea, New Zealand, and Singapore in the region. On March 31, 2020, the Fed announced the FIMA repo facility. This new dollar facility allows foreign central banks with accounts at the Fed to temporarily convert their US treasury securities into dollars. Additional agreements may be needed between emerging market economies and global lenders of last resort such as the Fed and the IMF.

Third, regional cooperation for financial safety net arrangements through the Chiang Mai Initiative Multilateralization (CMIM) and additional regional bilateral swap lines can also bolster market confidence. The CMIM and a further strengthening of its capacity can shore up defense against dollar liquidity shortages. Strengthening the ASEAN+3

Macroeconomic Research Office (AMRO) surveillance capacity would further help detect and prevent buildups of vulnerabilities. Adequate foreign-exchange reserve holdings help support market confidence and contribute to financial stability. But the region's policymakers may consider expanding the reserve pool and/or participating members to enhance the regional capacity to provide dollar liquidity support during times of crisis.

Fourth, in the medium- to long-term, the development of vibrant local currency bond markets can help address the currency and maturity mismatches of Asian financial systems. The ASEAN+3 Asian Bond Markets Initiative (ABMI) helps promote the development of regional capital markets. Greater availability of local currency long-term securities can reduce the need for short-term dollar funding needs.

Lastly, the persistent and large demand for US dollar funding by non-US banks reveals some fundamental issues of the international monetary system. It relies on the US dollar as a credit-based reserve currency while the use of a single national currency as an international reserve currency is inherently unstable. The global rush for the US dollar at any sign of market turbulence will easily swamp dollar funding markets, no matter how big daily foreign exchange swap transactions may be. Efforts to redesign the global financial architecture should embrace renewed discussion of the reform of the international reserve system to include multiple currency units down the road.

© 2020 World Scientific Publishing Company
https://doi.org/10.1142/9789811229381_0018

Chapter 18

The Impact of COVID-19 on Asia and the Future of Global Supply Chains

Bert Hofman

East Asian Institute, National University Singapore

The world economy is gradually coming out of the great lockdown. Overall, East Asian countries seem to have done better in managing the epidemic than most Western countries. The differences between East and West are so large that a data issue, which undoubtedly play a role,[1] cannot be the full explanation (Figure 1). Some countries that, according to the Global Health Index were among the most prepared in the world, such as the US, the UK, and Sweden fared poorly compared to Asian countries.[2] Deaths from COVID-19 per million and number of cases per million is a

---

[1] Data reliability and testing is playing a role, and in particular data for China are less reliable. Countries differ in the way they register deaths, and also differ in levels of testing, which makes diagnostics and COVID-19 patient numbers more reliable. Numbers on excess deaths are more reliable than deaths, but are only available for a small number of countries. Our World in Data provides data that indicate differences in testing per country, which would give an indication on the reliability of the number of patients. https://ourworldindata.org/coronavirus-data.

[2] GHS Index, https://www.ghsindex.org/.

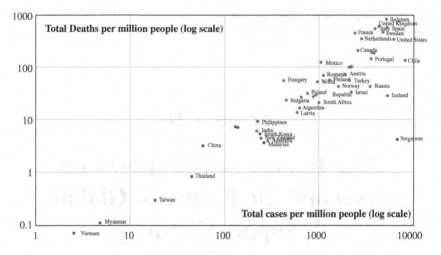

Figure 1.   Deaths per million and cases per million in select countries.

Source: Our World in Data based on European Centre for Disease Prevention and Control (ECDC). Data as of May 29, 2000. Vietnam registered zero deaths, which cannot be displayed on a log scale.

factor 10 to a 100 higher in Western countries than in East Asian countries. Some structural factors such as age and co-morbidities can explain some of the difference. Nevertheless, a lot seems to come down on the different approaches governments around the globe took, how fast they took action, and how rapid people changed their behavior, even before government measures made them do so.

Past epidemics inoculated several Asian countries. SARS, H1N1 and MERS were still fresh in the minds of the people, and in the contingency plans, the organization and attitudes of policymakers. Taiwan, famously, started monitoring visitors from the mainland on travel history and symptoms of the disease on January 1, 2020, the day after China had reported the new virus to the WHO. Neighboring countries followed soon after, and escalated measures as the situation changed. Even so, the US was prepared as well, through H1N1 and Ebola, which were both well managed in the recent past. As recently as October 2018 the US had reviewed its procedures to fight epidemics, and found them wanting.[3] This time was

---

[3] The National Biodefence Strategy elaborates on the steps needed to secure the US from biological incidents including epidemics, https://www.whitehouse.gov/wp-content/

different, unfortunately. The Institut Montaigne has done a very good summary of the East Asian experience, and the East Asian Institute analyzed a number of countries' experience in-depth.[4]

In contrast to expectations, some of the poorer countries in the world have taken some of the strictest mitigation measures to control the virus. An economic approach to measures (see for instance, Barnett-Howell and Mobarak[5]) would expect policymakers to tradeoff the benefit of lives saved with restrictive measures and lockdowns, versus the cost to the economy. Elderly have less long to live, so the value of their lives saved counts for less than the young. At the same time the impact of COVID-19 on the elderly is more severe. In poorer countries, where people live in more crowded places, and it is harder to protect them from economic hardship because social safety nets are less developed, the effectiveness of lockdown measures may be more limited, and thus theory would expect less strict lockdown.

None of that seems to hold: the countries with the strictest lockdown measures are India, the Philippines, and Vietnam. In contrast, rich countries such as Sweden (and the UK initially) chose only mildly mitigating measures, accepting the fact that they ended up with some of the highest death rates. Similarly, some states in the US feel more strongly about personal freedoms, and accept a higher death toll. It is not only government measures that determine people's behaviors, though. People adjust their behavior in response to the disease and the severity as well as to government measures, as Bill Maloney and Temel Taskin of the World Bank have shown (Figure 2). Even more striking, there seems to be little

---

uploads/2018/09/National-Biodefense-Strategy.pdf. The United States Health Security National Action Plan provides more details on steps needed to increase preparedness, https://www.phe.gov/Preparedness/international/Documents/jee-nap-508.pdf.

[4] Mathieu Duchâtel, François Godement and Viviana Zhu. April 2020. Fighting COVID-19: East Asian Responses to the Pandemic, https://www.institutmontaigne.org/en/publications/fighting-covid-19-east-asian-responses-pandemic; EAI Background Briefs (2020), https://research.nus.edu.sg/eai/eai-background-briefs-2020/.

[5] Zachary Barnett-Howell and Ahmed Mushfiq Mobarak. April 2020. Should Low-Income Countries Impose the Same Social Distancing Guidelines as Europe and North America to Halt the Spread of COVID-19? https://som.yale.edu/sites/default/files/mushifiq-howell-v2.pdf.

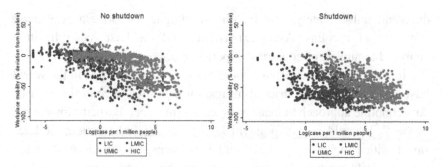

Figure 2. Workplace mobility and effects of shutdown versus caseload.

Source: Bill Maloney and Temel Taskin, "Voluntary vs mandated social distancing and economic activity during COVID-19", CEPR Policy Portal, https://voxeu.org/article/covid-social-distancing-driven-mostly-voluntary-demobilisation, accessed June 23, 2020.

difference between behaviors in low- and middle-income countries and high-income countries.

On individual behavior, there seems to be a marked difference in the attitude towards masks. Advice, including from the WHO and governments has been confusing, and was in part driven by the fact that there were not enough masks for everyone, so reserving them for medical personnel made sense. Even now, though, with masks abundantly available, there is a stark contrast between countries in the likelihood that people wear them (Figure 3).

The early response in East Asia seems to have paid off in terms of limiting damage to the economies. In fact, Emerging East Asia is the only region which, according to the World Bank's latest projections, will show positive growth in 2020 (Table 1). And the reversal in growth projections compared to January has been least sharp than in other parts of the world.

A key question on policymakers' minds is whether there will be lasting damage to world trade and global value chains (GVC). GVC trade rapidly expanded in the two decades after 2000. In part, this was driven by China's entry in the WTO, but deeper integration in Europe, among other factors due to the introduction of the Euro, also boosted GVC trade (Figure 4). The global financial crisis in 2008/9 sharply reduced trade as a share of GDP, a reduction that was led by a drop in Global Value Chain Trade — trade in goods that crosses more than one border. Trade bounced

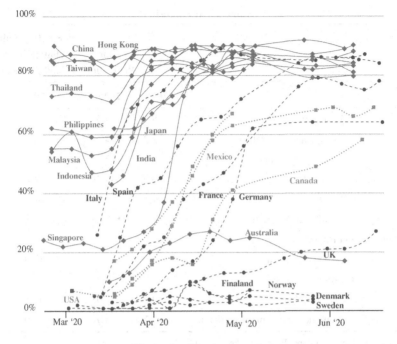

Figure 3.   Wearing a mask.

Source: Yougov. "Personal measures taken to avoid COVID-19", https://yougov.co.uk/topics/international/articles-reports/2020/03/17/personal-measures-taken-avoid-covid-19, accessed June 23, 2020.
Note: Percentage of people who say they are wearing a mask in public.

Table 1.   GDP growth projections (percent change).

		June Projection	Percentage point change from 1/2020 projection
	2019	**2020**	**2020**
World	**2.4**	**−5.2**	**−7.7**
Advanced economies	**1.6**	**−7.0**	**−8.4**
United States	2.3	−6.1	−7.9
Euro Area	1.2	−9.1	−10.1
Japan	0.7	−6.1	−6.8
Emerging market and developing economies	**3.5**	**−2.5**	**−6.6**

(*Continued*)

Table 1.   (*Continued*)

	2019	June Projection 2020	Percentage point change from 1/2020 projection 2020
East Asia and Pacific	5.9	0.5	−5.2
Europe and Central Asia	2.2	−4.7	−7.3
Latin America and the Caribbean	0.8	−7.2	−9.0
Middle East and North Africa	−0.2	−4.2	−6.6
South Asia	4.7	−2.7	−8.2
Sub-Saharan Africa	2.2	−2.8	−5.8
Memorandum items:			
World trade volume	0.8	−13.4	−15.3
Commodity prices			
Oil price	−10.2	−47.9	−42.5
Non-energy commodity price index	−4.2	−5.9	−6.0

Source: World Bank, Global Economic Prospects, June 2020.

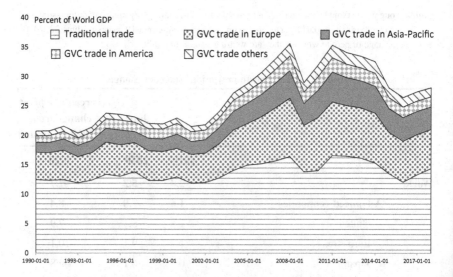

Figure 4.   World trade and global value chain trade.

Source: OECD Economic Outlook 107 database; UNCTAD-Eora database; and OECD calculations.
Note: Traditional trade includes products entirely produced in one country and consumed in another one. GVC trade includes all backward and forward linkages of each country in the region.

back after the crisis, but since then, trade intensity of GDP has been on the decline. The nature of growth since the financial crisis explains some: it was driven by government spending and consumption, less by investment, which is more trade and GVC intensive.

In addition, though, the drivers of past growth in GVC trade — improved communication, lower transport costs, lower tariffs, and cost differences with countries such as China — have largely played out their role (see the World Development Report 2020 for an elaboration of this argument[6]). Moreover, China has started to onshore more and more of the value chain it is involved in, and many suppliers that previously were located outside of China moved onshore. This reduced the share of trade that is counted as GVC trade.

Whether the COVID-19 shock will accelerate these trends remains to be seen. Early on in the COVID-19 pandemic, when the spread of the virus was confined to China and its Asian neighbors, there was considerable fear that the epidemic would cause considerable supply constraints. China had shut down its economy to contain the virus and the analogy was that of major natural disasters like the Japan earthquake or Thailand floods, which had affected supply chains worldwide. A "China+1" strategy, already making its rounds in world's boardrooms because of the trade war, now seemed more necessary than ever because of supply chain vulnerabilities from China.

Fast forward to today, and talk about supply chain vulnerabilities is still there, but like the virus, it is everywhere, not just China. The epidemic may still lead to changes in supply chains, and the production of some sensitive goods such as medical equipment and medicine may be "reshored" to the countries that needed them at the peak of the pandemic. But for most goods, an increase in the amount of inventory held will likely be enough to absorb future shocks, and just in time production will have to change. Resilience to events such as epidemics is likely to be a more prominent factor in future investment decisions, though the question is to what extent this will be to the disadvantage of Asian countries.

---

[6]The World Bank. 2020. World Development Report 2020: Trading for Development in the Age of Global Value Chains, https://www.worldbank.org/en/publication/wdr2020.

According to the CPB World Trade Monitor, the impact of COVID-19 on world trade was sharply negative, but less so than during the global financial crisis. By May 2020, world trade in manufacturing goods was down 17% y-o-y in volume, after which recovery set in. By August 2020, trade was only down 6%. In contrast, by January 2009, trade volumes were down 19% y-o-y, and it took a full year to recover. For some countries, the second quarter of 2020 was particularly bad, with France (–42% y-o-y) and South Africa (–48% y-o-y) experiencing the largest decline in April. In contrast, China, which had its peak decline in January–February at 17% showed only a modest 3.3% decline (y-o-y) in May exports.

For countries in East Asia, the demand side is now the constraint, not the supply side. One factor of good luck was that the virus hit economies just before Lunar New Year. In a normal year, production is ramped up before this event, as key East Asian economies virtually close down for two to three weeks of holidays. This could explain in part the fact that China's trade with other East Asian countries fell considerably less than with other countries and actually increased with ASEAN (Figure 5): China increasingly exports intermediaries to those countries, and there seems to have been no shortage thereof.

Aside from COVID-19, though, the other factor affecting GVCs and trade is the US–China trade war. COVID-19 itself has sharply increased tensions between the two nations, but for now neither side has said it would shelf the January 2020 Phase I trade deal. Nevertheless, the trade war has sharply reduced bilateral trade, much more so than the general decline in trade the countries experienced. In 2019, imports of the US fell by 2% overall, whereas imports from China fell by 17% (Figure 5). In the first quarter of 2020, this trend accelerated: whereas US imports declined by 5% overall, imports from China fell by 28%. China's exports show a similar pattern for the first 4 months of 2020: total exports fell by 6.4%, while those to the US fell by 15.5%.

As for China's imports, the focus is on the commitments China has made in the Phase I Deal to increase imports in specific categories to the tune of some $180 billion this year. The US and China have both reconfirmed their commitment to the deal, despite the sharp exchanges between the countries on COVID-19. For now, though, China is well behind

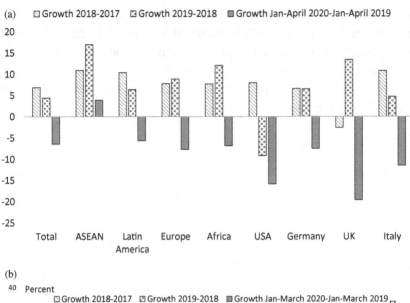

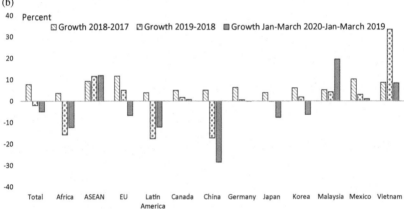

Figure 5. Trade war or COVID-19?

Source: China customs via CEIC data; Author's calculations.

schedule as Chad Bown of PIIE shows in his commitment tracker.[7] China may catch up on imports later in the year, but delays in trade because of COVID-19 will make it harder to do so, and perhaps not timely enough

---

[7] Chad P. Bown. August 2020. US-China phase one tracker: China's purchases of US goods, https://www.piie.com/research/piie-charts/us-china-phase-one-tracker-chinas-purchases-us-goods.

for an election year. Already, the tariffs imposed in the past two years are putting pressure on the GVCs anchored in China, as does a rapidly expanding "entities list" and other restrictions on trade in US technology with Chinese entities. More trade policy moves could aggravate this, and it will be policies, not viruses, that will determine the shape of Global Value Chains to come.

© 2020 World Scientific Publishing Company
https://doi.org/10.1142/9789811229381_0019

Chapter 19

International Trade Has Suffered a One-Two Punch: Can It Recover After COVID-19?

Davin Chor[1]

Tuck School of Business, Dartmouth College; National Bureau of Economic Research; Asian Bureau of Finance and Economic Research

At the start of 2020, international trade was already under a protectionist cloud. Rising trade tensions between the US and the rest of the world, particularly China, had been in the economic headlines for three years, with US imports from China shrinking by a dramatic 17.7% between 2018–2019.[2] Despite the Phase 1 deal signed between the two countries on 15 January 2020, few observers saw this as the last bump in the road in this tariff war.

The coronavirus (COVID-19) pandemic has landed an unexpected and unwelcome follow-up blow to the gut, and world trade has now been left reeling like a boxer from a swift one-two punch.

---

[1] Davin Chor is Associate Professor and Globalization Chair at the Tuck School of Business at Dartmouth, a Research Associate at the NBER, and a Fellow of the ABFER.
[2] According to the US Census Bureau, US imports from China totaled US\$539.7 billion in 2018 and US\$452.2 billion in 2019, in non-seasonally adjusted terms. https://www.census.gov/foreign-trade/balance/c5700.html.

COVID-19 is first and foremost a public health crisis. Our thoughts and prayers should rightly be with those who have been infected, and with medical workers and first-responders around the world. So, mulling over the impact of the pandemic on international trade may seem like we are getting ahead of ourselves. But make no mistake, the imprint of COVID-19 on global trade flows is already being felt.

According to data released by the US Census Bureau, US imports stood at US$178.3 billion (in non-seasonally adjusted terms) in February 2020, a 9.7% decrease relative to the US$196.4 billion recorded in the previous month.[3] This was driven by a stunning contraction in imports from China, from US$33.3 billion in January 2020 to US$22.8 billion in February 2020. Although US imports as a whole bounced back somewhat to US$194.4 billion in March 2020, US imports from China continued their slide, dropping further to US$19.8 billion in March 2020. In other words, US purchases of goods from China have slipped more than 40%, and this has been made up only partially by US imports from its other major trade partners such as the EU and the UK.

Much of this decline reflects of course the severe shock to supply chains, as the pandemic peaked in mainland China in February 2020. As China sought to aggressively shut down the spread of the coronavirus, factory shifts were shortened or even completely shuttered. However, the concern for global trade now extends beyond the impact of COVID-19 on the supply side. Global demand has sagged as the EU and the US have slipped into an economic slowdown and unemployment has risen, the inevitable consequence of the drastic stay-at-home measures necessary to "flatten the curve" of infections. Moreover, measures taken to avert the spread of the coronavirus — such as the trimming of staff numbers to maintain a safe distance between co-workers — can be expected to slow down international shipments of goods through port facilities and distribution centers.

Just as the pandemic has medically afflicted some segments of the population more than others, its effect is likely to be uneven too across

---

[3] The corresponding decline in year-on-year terms, i.e., relative to the US$185.9 billion of imports in February 2019, was 4.2%. On the other hand, US exports rose but only modestly to US$132.1 billion in February 2020, from US$129.0 billion in January 2020. https://www.census.gov/foreign-trade/balance/c0015.html.

different tradable goods industries. Flows of medical equipment and supplies have been buoyed, as has the demand for home electronic products (by families now confined indoors). On the other hand, purchases of big-ticket consumer durables such as cars has stalled.

It is tempting to try to paint an optimistic scenario of where world trade may be headed: Once the worst of the pandemic has passed, perhaps trade flows will bounce back as supply chain managers simply press the re-start button to meet a swift recovery in global demand. But that would be far too sanguine a scenario in my view. There are clear signs amidst the ongoing crisis response that this episode will have long-lasting repercussions for patterns of global trade and production, as well as the conduct of trade policy. I raise three observations below that should be of concern both to academic researchers and policy practitioners.

First, there has been a frantic scramble by governments — and even by individual hospitals — to secure supplies of essential medical items, such as personal protective equipment (PPE), face masks, ventilators, chemical reagents for test-kits, and so on. This has already prompted calls for restrictions to be placed on trade flows of such goods. Witness for example the pressure applied by the Trump administration on 3M to restrict its exports of N95 masks to Canada and Latin America,[4] notwithstanding Canada's position as one of the US' closest trading partners. Such calls are likely to get more frequent and voluminous, especially if the pandemic were to drag on, with subsequent waves of infection prompting repeated surges in demand for these essential goods.

One can argue that it is only natural for a country's government to try to secure such supplies for its own citizens. But the resort to unilateral trade policies to achieve this end is a slippery slope. What is to restrain a creeping expansion of the list of items deemed to be vital for national security? If N95 masks are fair game, why not restrict trade in test-kits, drugs, or perhaps even an eventual vaccine on similar grounds? The concern here is that the world trade landscape will become increasingly protectionist and siloed. This is even though the opposite course of action — the removal of trade barriers and the expansion of cooperation — would instead help to boost economies of scale in the global production of these

---

[4] BBC. "Coronavirus: US 'wants 3M to end mask exports to Canada and Latin America'." April 3, 2020. https://www.bbc.com/news/world-us-canada-52161032.

essential items. Such trade restrictions moreover raise a whole host of ethical issues related to developing countries' access to life-saving resources, even as they face the brunt of the global pandemic.

Second, this pandemic will force firms and countries to reassess their exposure to global supply chain disruptions. I would be surprised if such discussions have not already been triggered in earnest in most multinational corporations. Prior to COVID-19, few would have foreseen an event catastrophic enough to simultaneously shut down factories in China and close virtually all major border crossings to short-term travel. Yet this is exactly the state of affairs that materialized in February 2020. Some firms in the service sector have been better able to adapt, by making a transition to remote operations and telecommuting. But firms in the manufacturing sector — that depend on physical flows of parts and components for their production operations — do not have this luxury. Already, there is talk that this pandemic could lead manufacturing firms to back away from offshoring,[5] to instead bring home production of key inputs, in order to avoid disruptions from possible border closures. At the very least, I would expect that firms will actively seek to diversify the sources of their inputs, to reduce their dependence on supplies from any single country. This could even prompt companies to adopt technologies such as 3D printing, which could make it more feasible for production to be concentrated in fewer locations. The cross-border fragmentation of manufacturing activity that we have seen for several decades seems due for a pause as companies now rethink their sourcing strategies.

One should expect too that governments will get in on this act, to champion the need to retain more production within their borders. Country governments in Europe and the US have found themselves exposed during this pandemic by their lack of domestic manufacturing capacity for critical medical equipment such as ventilators. With unemployment on the rise, particularly in the US, it would come as no surprise if calls for more tariffs were to intensify, on the grounds that this will help to shore up domestic manufacturing capabilities and retain jobs in that sector. That this timing will coincide with the height of campaigning for the 2020 US

---

[5] BBC. "Will coronavirus reverse globalization?" April 2, 2020. https://www.bbc.com/news/business-52104978.

presidential election only raises the likelihood that tariffs will be in the spotlight once again. Ever since the Smoot–Hawley tariffs during the Great Depression, there has been a tendency for countries to turn to protectionism as a "solution" in the aftermath of major economic downturns. This downturn brought about by COVID-19 is shaping up to be no different.

Third, the coronavirus pandemic could further complicate cross-country economic relations that were already under strain entering 2020. Take the prominent case of US–China trade ties. At one level, there is a recognition that both the US and China have an interest in maintaining a working trade relationship that results in a win–win bargain: Now that China appears to have gotten over the worst of COVID-19, it has become a key exporter of emergency medical supplies to the US (and the EU). However, this bilateral relationship remains fraught with uncertainty, as China remains an easy bogeyman to criticize and pin the blame on for the coronavirus outbreak. This has heightened the risk of missteps in how US–China trade ties evolve moving forward. Let us not forget too that the pandemic has shaken other economic relationships that were once thought to be rock solid. The US–Canada land border was shut in March 2020. Likewise, EU countries have shut their borders — an unimaginable scenario just months ago — to stem the spread of the virus, calling into question the notion of European solidarity.

In short, there is a real and pressing concern that the COVID-19 pandemic will accentuate the return of protectionism. In the extreme, it may even undo the progress made towards cross-country economic integration over the past decades. How businesses and countries choose to respond will have far-reaching implications for the direction in which the conduct of world trade and global production are headed.

© 2020 World Scientific Publishing Company
https://doi.org/10.1142/9789811229381_0020

Chapter 20

COVID-19 in the Global Production Network

Ben Charoenwong

NUS Business School, National University of Singapore

Not only do firms around the world rely on many Asian companies for crucial supplies, Asian countries also represent a substantial component of global demand. An October 2019 report by the International Monetary Fund shows Asia represented 70.9% of global economic growth in 2019, with China alone contributing 39% and India contributing around 16%.[1] Both countries are important supply chain sources for companies all around the world.

Why is COVID-19 Different from SARS?

Beyond the differences between the COVID-19 pandemic and the SARS epidemic from an epidemiology standpoint, the economic context has also changed. In 2003, SARS decreased China's GDP by 0.5 percentage points while the rest of the Asia Pacific region did not suffer

---

[1] International Monetary Fund. (October 22, 2019). Prolonged Uncertainty Weighs on Asia's Economy. *IMF NEWS*, retrieved from https://www.imf.org/en/News/Articles/2019/10/18/na102319-prolonged-uncertainty-weighs-on-asias-economy.

long-term impacts. To say the least, there have been several transformations since then.

Global trade has expanded dramatically both in terms of volume as well as complexity, from $7.9 trillion in goods and services in 2002 to $19.7 trillion in 2018. China's share of world GDP has grown from 4% to 16% today. Not only is China the largest buyer of soy beans and copper, it is also a large source of revenues for the high-tech sector in America. For example, in 2019, China represented almost 50% of Qualcomm's revenues. Meanwhile, Apple relies on Foxconn as a crucial parts supplier and customers in China represented 15% of its sales.

Now, a negative shock to China's production level goes beyond an idiosyncratic shock felt by a handful of firms, but percolates through the global production networks. Further, even if China contains and eliminates the virus, as COVID-19 travels around the world, what started as a short-run supply chain disruption may evolve into longer-term depressed global demand.

Lessons on Costs Versus Resilience

Firms face a fundamental tradeoff in terms of costs of production and resiliency of its supply chain. On the one hand, low costs of production in Asia improve a firm's profit margins. Volume discounts and the specialization of inputs incentivize firms to concentrate supply chain relationships to a handful of manageable key suppliers. In addition, "just in time" operations and lean production permit firms to hold less inventory which can further amplify supply chain disruptions.

On the other hand, holding additional inventory and supply chain redundancy improve the resilience of a firm's production process to idiosyncratic production shocks. For example, my research with Jing Wu and Miaozhe Han from the Chinese University of Hong Kong finds that in response to the US–China trade war that was the precursor to the COVID-19 pandemic, firms appear to have taken costly actions to move their supply chains closer to their customer bases following heightened periods of trade policy uncertainty.[2]

---

[2]Ben Charoenwong, Miaozhe Han, Jing Wu. (February 7, 2020). Not Coming Home: Trade and Economic Policy Uncertainty in American Supply Chain Networks. Retrieved from https://papers.ssrn.com/sol3/papers.cfm?abstract_id=3533827.

Unfortunately, unlike the concerns surrounding bilateral trade policy, the COVID-19 pandemic is not diversifiable. While supply chain redundancy can mitigate production disruptions at the start of the pandemic, few remain unscathed as the virus spreads around the globe.

The pain of a virus-induced global lockdown is immediately felt in service-oriented industries, such as aviation, tourism, F&B, and entertainment. However, even if firms in other sectors are able to weather the short-run demand freeze, as inventories of crucial parts deplete, manufacturing firms may also see production lines halt.

Contrary to the impact felt through supply chain networks, firms whose business models involve establishing an online platform or a market in fact see a demand increase. In fact, current Chinese tech giants Alibaba and Tencent both grew partly due to the SARS experience pushing commerce online.[3]

The study of global production networks will likely be of more importance as the world witnesses the wide-ranging effects of correlated supply disruptions. For example, the current mandatory reporting standard means that many firms may not even know their own supply chain exposures.[4] The burden on regulators would be to strike an appropriate balance between proprietary information of firms versus transparency for risk mitigation. As financial economists have adopted more careful analysis of studying the inter-banking network after the Global Financial Crisis in 2008, economists may further extend those tools to study the impact of firm-level production networks.

---

[3] Jane Zhang and Coco Feng. (March 7, 2020) Will the Coronavirus Crisis, Like Sars, Give Birth to the Next Big Thing in China Tech? South China Morning Post, retrieved from https://www.scmp.com/tech/big-tech/article/3073961/will-coronavirus-crisis-sars-give-birth-next-big-thing-china-tech.

[4] For example, the SFAS Accounting Requirement in the United States requires firms to disclose geographical regions contributing at least 10% of sales and also the identity of key customers who represent at least 10% of sales.

© 2020 World Scientific Publishing Company
https://doi.org/10.1142/9789811229381_0021

Chapter 21

Post–COVID-19 Reconfiguration of the Global Value Chains and China[1]

Hanming Fang* and Bernard Yeung[†]

*University of Pennsylvania;
Asian Bureau of Finance and Economic Research
[†]NUS Business School, National University of Singapore;
Asian Bureau of Finance and Economic Research

The iPhone was designed at Apple's headquarters in Cupertino, California, but its parts were made by suppliers in 43 countries and six continents via an incredibly complex supply chain. The global supply chain is the epitome of the intensive drive for efficiency, necessitated by fierce global competition. China emerged as the center of the global supply chain and the *de facto* "factory of the world" after it joined the World Trade Organization in 2001.

The configuration of production facilities is based on a global model whose primary objective is to increase efficiency. Many considerations enter into the calculus that shapes the global supply chain. First and

---

[1]This commentary has appeared in Vox China on June 10, 2020, and also in ABFER "2020 Pandemic commentary".

foremost, the configuration of the global supply chain aims to minimize costs, including the labor cost, the cost of transporting the components for final assembly, and the assembly cost itself. It is no coincidence that the global supply chain has increasingly consolidated production in economies with abundant capable labor, better infrastructure, and lax environmental regulations, primarily those based in China, Taiwan, Vietnam, or other Asian economies. Second, the global supply chain tends to locate the production facilities close to the consumers of the final products. The emergence of the huge Chinese middle class and their purchasing power further enhances China as the leading destination for foreign direct investment. These two factors combine to make China the central link of the global value chain.

Of course, cost minimization is not the only consideration for the configuration of the global supply chain. When a firm like Apple sources iPhone components from 200 suppliers over 800 production facilities in numerous countries, it must manage a multitude of risks judiciously. These include mundane risks such as exchange rate risks and potential delays in the delivery of key components. Global value chain management handles these risks with remarkable effectiveness via hedging, stockpiling of inventories of key components, and multi-sourcing.

COVID-19 Does Not Change the Fundamentals

COVID-19 certainly disrupts the global value chain, and we are interested in how COVID-19 may reconfigure it. When facing bona fide uncertainty, it is useful to take a step back to understand how the fundamentals, as described above, shape the future. Some factors that made China into the factory of the world had already been evolving before the COVID-19 pandemic.

There are both negative and positive developments. First, labor costs have risen sharply from 2011, when China reached the Lewis turning point due to several converging forces, including the depletion of the surplus labor from its agricultural sector and the rapidly changing demographics induced by the three decades of the one-child policy. "Made in China" is not so cheap anymore. Second, decades of rapid economic growth with lax environmental regulations inevitably resulted in unbreathable air in many Chinese metropolitan areas. Green and sustainable development has become the mantra of the new growth model in China. Environmental costs of producing in China, which were unaccounted for in the race for China to become the factory of the world, are now finally factored in as a part of the cost, as they should. On the positive side, the elusive purchasing power of the Chinese middle class has finally become a reality. China is now the world's largest automobile market. The Chinese consumer market is about to overtake the United States as the world's largest.

Even though the labor cost in China has risen sharply in recent years, at least in the major manufacturing centers in Eastern and Southern China, China's vast Central and Western provinces still have inexpensive labor and affordable living costs. Fast infrastructure development makes them attractive production locations to serve both Chinese and global consumers. The US–China trade war from 2018 injected geopolitical uncertainty into the picture. Many firms contemplating moving their production lines from Guangdong or Jiangsu provinces to Western China may scale back their plans with a sharpened focus on serving only the China market. However, Southeast Asian countries such as Vietnam, Cambodia, and Indonesia seemed to be a safer production location as a result of the US–China trade tensions. China may not feel the impact in the short term, as it still enjoys many advantages such as agglomeration efficiency and superb infrastructure, but in the medium term China cannot ignore the impact from the US–China conflicts on the global supply chain relocations.

COVID-19 Heightens Worries, Reveals China's Strengths, But Expedites Ongoing Changes

The above-mentioned factors were already serving to loosen the screws that held China at the center of the global value chain before the COVID-19 pandemic. What will the impact of the pandemic be on the changing landscape of the global value chain a decade from now?

The biggest revelation from the pandemic is the importance of supply chain robustness. A survey conducted by the Institute For Supply

Chain Management in March 2020 found that nearly 75% of companies reported supply chain disruptions in one form or another due to coronavirus-related transportation restrictions, and the figure is expected to rise further over the next few weeks. In addition, the survey also found that almost half of the companies lacked any semblance of a contingency plan for their supply chain disruption.

The Chinese political system has shown its strength in controlling the pandemic. Once the government recognized that the novel coronavirus is highly contagious, with a rather high mortality rate, the powerful Chinese state machinery was in full force. It enforced strict lockdowns of the country's epicenters, facilitated rapid mobilization of resources to assist the epicenters, and implemented technology-based tracing of interpersonal contact to prevent new waves of outbreaks. Given its efficacy in battling this pandemic, or likely any future epidemic or pandemic, China would emerge as a desirable location for the global supply chain. Firms would obviously prefer to locate their factories in an area where disruption from the pandemic has a more limited duration.

However, this argument holds only if the global value chain remains centralized in one country — mainly China. The new recognition for the importance of supply chain resilience or robustness is likely to lead to regionalism in organizing global supply chains. By that, we mean that the global value chain will likely become multi-centered. That is, having *the* factory of the world will be replaced by having one factory for each region. Currently, China is *the* factory of the world. The regionalism of global supply chains will diminish the centrality of China in the global value chain.

The COVID-19 pandemic introduces no new forces in the reconfigurations of the global value chain; it simply intensifies the existing forces of heightened geopolitical risks that the US–China trade war unleashed. There was already talk of supply chain diversification by building redundant capacity, sourcing from multiple producers in multiple locations, re-clustering the network of component production/sourcing around major consumption centers, and politically forced decoupling, leading to the development of multiple manufacturing clusters. The COVID-19 pandemic will simply reinforce this dynamic, and expedite this reconfiguration.

Economics is Key

However, ultimately, companies act according to economics. This means China will remain one of the centers of the global value chain because of the many advantages that made China into the current factory of the world. Rising labor costs notwithstanding, the looming automation wave will allow China to remain cost-competitive. The enormous Chinese domestic market will grow larger as Chinese policymakers deepen reforms — such as a better social safety net, affordable housing, rural land reform — that will both expand the size of the Chinese middle class and make those individuals more willing to spend rather than save. The sheer size of the Chinese market will keep and further attract China-based manufacturing.

We should also recognize the efficiency-robustness tradeoff in supply chain regionalism, or diversification. Not exercising comparative advantage is inefficient, as is decoupling and building excess capacity. Regionalism also means losing economies of scale, which results in fewer incentives for innovation effort. Talk of sourcing all medical supplies domestically may over-estimate the need for robustness at the expense of efficiency, or may simply be politicians' paranoia. Stockpiling could have achieved medical supply safeguards without sacrificing production efficiency. An even better solution to future global health crises would seem to be creating a global health organization to play a similar role to the International Monetary Fund and provide medical supplies to countries of need. We hope that the world will not take away the wrong lessons from the words of paranoid politicians.

What Should China Be Wary Of?

To what extent should China be concerned about the coming shift to regionalism in the global supply chain? Many people are concerned about the consequences of unemployment. Indeed short-run adjustments are necessary, but the long-term equilibrium unemployment rate is determined by a labor market's ability to adjust to market changes, not by trade balance. After all, the Chinese labor force is rapidly aging and shrinking. If anything, automation, which is a response to the aging workforce and technological progress, is the more important concern when it comes to employment than the shift of the global supply chain. The Chinese domestic market is huge and most of it is yet untapped. The concern in China is about a looming labor shortage and thus the need to take up smart responses, like automation, to meet production demand.

China has also become an important source of outbound foreign investment, so one may argue that losing inbound foreign direct investment is not as much of a concern. On this point, we caution against this complacency. Foreign direct investment as a result of multinationals locating their supply chain in China should get more credit for playing an important positive role in raising China's economic efficiency. Beyond employment and growth, foreign direct investment brought important and large positive spill overs to the productivity of domestic firms via two channels: (i) showcased innovative technology and management, and (ii) intensified market competition.

Without foreign firms, Chinese domestic firms, whether private or not, may play a very different competition game. The winners are less likely the fittest, but more likely the most connected. The competition from foreign firms in China puts pressure on Chinese domestic firms to improve corporate governance, both at the company and the market level. As more multinationals move their supply chains out of China, there will be less competition in the market for corporate control, and less competition for investment opportunities. Worse yet, the connected firms may use the opportunity to slow down meaningful improvement in supply-side management in the country.

The de-coupling phenomenon has negative ramifications in markets with less-than-fully developed market and legal institutions. For China, this is the more worrisome implication of the post–COVID-19 global supply chain reconfiguration. It is the most urgent time to intensify the advancement of market and legal institutions in China to ensure that the most productive firms emerge as the winners in the race for market shares.

Part V

Concluding Remarks — A Post–COVID-19 World

© 2020 World Scientific Publishing Company
https://doi.org/10.1142/9789811229381_0022

Chapter 22

Post–COVID-19, How Will We Be Better?

Danny Quah[1]

Lee Kuan Yew School of Public Policy,
National University of Singapore

More so than past financial crises, the pandemic is a spur to societies to focus on the really big tradeoffs in life.

During the Great Plague of London of 1665, as a social-distancing measure, Cambridge University temporarily sent everyone home. One of the university's students, Isaac Newton, took literally "Work from Home". During the lockdown, sitting in his family's Lincolnshire house, 23-year-old Newton invented calculus, and discovered the laws of optics and light, and of universal gravitation.

None of these research advances had anything to do with the bubonic plague then ravaging England and eventually killing a quarter of London's population. However, by the time Cambridge re-opened in 1667, the

---

[1] Dean, and Li Ka Shing Professor in Economics, Lee Kuan Yew School of Public Policy. An edited and abbreviated version was published as: Quah, D. 2020. "Could it be time to swop fast car for slower, sturdier one?", Straits Times (23 April), https://www.straitstimes. com/opinion/could-it-be-time-to-swop-fast-car-for-slower-sturdier-one.

world had come to understand itself better, and would soon be primed for a scientific and industrial revolution unprecedented in scale and scope.

In the year 2020, how should the world change post–COVID-19? Will we all just go back to business as usual? What lessons do we need to learn from this pandemic?

After all, a crisis is a terrible thing to waste.

What makes this episode different, from say the 2008 Global Financial Crisis or the 1997 Asian Financial Crisis, that it might be realistic to expect change in all the world as a result of what we're now going through?

Upfront and Personal

The key feature of the COVID-19 outbreak is how it engages individuals in global society at a real, personal level. In this pandemic, ordinary people see palpable risk exposure for each of themselves: they know they will die or become gravely ill, unless they behave a certain way. Each individual is empowered to take actions that can forestall their personal sickness and mortality. People can, of course, choose to act otherwise, but retribution — whether it's legal sanction, debilitating illness, or death from disease — is both swift and likely. With COVID-19, individual mechanisms of cause and effect are made transparent and immediate.

Sure, it is the social behavior of millions of ordinary people that will determine how the pandemic unfolds. But everybody counts.

For Singapore and Hong Kong and other parts of East Asia, the 2003 SARS outbreak shared these features: here, political and social systems changed as a result. In the rest of the world the SARS pandemic ended too quickly so its policy lessons were muted, and change was not deep. Living through pandemics changes people and political systems.

Other kinds of crises are different. Certainly, the 2008 Global Financial Crisis (GFC) had substantial impact on individuals. But individual empowerment and responsibility in a financial crisis have levels that are diminished or delayed in time. In terms of responsibility, individuals might see a link from a reckless investment decision years ago. But the causal mechanism is shrouded in financial collateralization or other obscure innovation, or misalignment of expectations. Also, a financial crisis is ultimately not the individual's fault, but that of something big: big banks, big corporations, big institutions. Reform coming out of a global financial crisis is needed but individuals hand that responsibility over to someone else, and often without genuine change then taking place. Big banks remain, post-2008 GFC, and many institutions engage in behavior not profoundly different from before. Asking for the system to change without deep individual engagement does not produce the same kind of real reform that a pandemic engenders.

With COVID-19 too there will be institutional accounting. But personal considerations matter for a pandemic in ways that other crises do not surface. Coming out of COVID-19, terms like social awareness and solidarity will no longer be just intellectual or political concepts, but ideas that ordinary people can see and feel vitally. Abstract tradeoffs such as privacy and individual rights versus authoritarian control will no longer be just what academics and ideologues debate. Instead, they will become concrete choices that people, post–COVID-19, routinely face in trading off increased bio-surveillance in return for elevated health security.

Based on observing Singapore's coronavirus responses, my guess is that economic life, among many other things, will need to change. On economics then, here are my conjectures for the world, post–COVID-19.

Economic Life — The Tradeoffs

Post–COVID-19, societies will realize why it is important to focus on the really big tradeoffs in life, and not sweat the small stuff. In Singapore there has long been a narrative on how simply getting richer should no longer be the goal of a population that is already middle-class. Here is the opportunity to act on that.

Think of economic life as a high-performance car, navigating a speed trial. There are two ways to do this. One is, you fine-tune every part of the car to within a nanometer of optimality. You cut excess baggage and trim all edges to perfection. You have a gleaming machine of global optimality that speeds along the smooth runway. The high-tech pieces receive the greatest attention, the large heavy pieces less so: inequality in care is high because that's how you make the parts fit together. The car's handling is wondrous, light as a bird. However, if that car hits a bump in the road that shouldn't be there, the whole thing falls apart: the pieces that have been fine-tuned in expectation of only smooth running suddenly misfire, and the entire machine grinds to a halt.

Alternatively, you put together a heavier, sturdier vehicle, not as fast as the other car. This one takes bumps in its stride — because it has not been so optimized for maximum speed on a perfectly smooth track — but then again it is not as quick when the runway is without blemish. Every part of the car matters — you provide more equal care across components — because it is the weakest link that needs to be strong.

The first car wins every time when everything runs as it should, because it is a machine of global optimality. Every component in the car knows its place and gets appropriately rewarded. The second car, however, will not blow up when things don't go so well. This car is heavily laden down with all kinds of back-up systems, that most of the time, apparently do nothing but just make the system less efficient. This second car's leading, high-tech parts don't always get the greatest attention, because it is the old-school, greasy stuff that will blow up if the road gets bumpy, and so those get better care too.

Now think back to the economy as if it were one of these cars. An economic strategy is not short-term efficient and profit-maximizing if it provides spare long-run excess capacity — in hospital beds and emergency wards, in food supply lines, agricultural production, or Internet connections and storage capacity. The rich are not going to become richer through installing spare back-up systems that are not optimized to whisker-thin margins for dealing with the normal ebb and flow of business. But if society is no longer about obsessively and incessantly raising material living standards, then it can certainly tolerate spare and idle capacity with built-in redundancies.

Healthcare and health security systems have long been known to be rife with problems of adverse selection and incomplete information, and cannot be driven to maximum economic efficiency. Building a health system that is robust with spare capacity is expensive, but not conceptually hard. It is when that system seeks to optimize out every single feature that adverse selection and other informational challenges become paramount. Societies should be satisfied with developing good health systems that, in the short-term, most of the time, seem idle with lots of spare capacity, and are not being run at optimal performance, but are actually gleaming, long-run models of complete responsiveness for those urgent crises that periodically but randomly hit society.

Extreme optimization is how the well-off continue to increase wealth. But extreme optimization comes by concentrating risk down to razor-thin shells. So, instead, post–COVID-19, let us make it a social imperative to emphasize redundancy and robustness in production systems. Ameliorate "economics of superstars" inequalities by eschewing global efficiency in favor of local resilience. This flattens the income distribution at the same time that it builds long-run social robustness.

This tradeoff between global efficiency and local robustness is everywhere, once you start looking.

The Weightless Economy

Across the world, cities and other urban agglomerations are dense with humanity and value creation. No other humanity-constructed economic scaffolding besides cities are lit when you view our planet from outer space. The greater the concentration, the higher the population and economic densities, and thus the higher the efficiency in producing material wealth. That higher efficiency from concentration makes for inequality across space, regions, geographies. But that higher concentration also makes for speed in transmitting viral infection. Post–COVID-19, social and economic systems will learn not to be maximally efficient in producing material wealth through urban concentration, when doing so only makes your society ever more susceptible to epidemic transmission.

If efficiency through concentration is no longer what economies seek, commercial real estate will lose its historical sparkle. So too will the need for mass transport systems wither. Decades ago, when the Internet was first being used for commercial purposes, writers noted that the so-called weightless economy entailed a shift in economic activity away from moving physical molecules to flipping 0-1 bits of logic. Telecommuting during COVID-19 over the Internet infrastructure has driven home to workers and businesses how such a weightless economy is not just feasible but actually life-saving. In protecting that new way of work and life, societies might have to build an entire second mirroring Internet to run parallel and be back-up to the first. But that is still a lot cheaper and less wasteful than building an entire second mass transit system to operate alongside the first.

Hedging Anchors

Maximal global efficiency in production calls for cross-country specialization. Post–COVID-19, societies need to balance off global efficiency with local resilience. As a proposition in logic alone, not every nation can be the best in the world at producing medication, personal protective equipment, rice and instant noodles, eggs, or toilet rolls. A lesson from COVID-19 is that societies will want to have some production capacity in all these. But nations need not refer to these industries as strategic — suggesting something geopolitically sinister — but instead simply as hedging anchors. Every nation should foster their own hedging anchors: It is fine to tolerate a bit of global inefficiency if doing so raises local resilience. A cross-nation network of semi-independent hedging anchors is no longer a supply chain and is not globally efficient, but will make the entire world more resilient.

The State and Market Shortcomings

Finally, COVID-19 has made clear how economic externalities are more widespread than previously thought. The key implication from this is that public policy needs to look out for and repair market shortcomings. Two cases illustrate this. First, in a world of externalities, you help yourself by helping others, because spill overs are rife. In Singapore many foreign workers live in crowded dormitories because these workers are poor. COVID-19 cases in these clusters have accounted for over 70% of all new cases in the past fourteen days. A national health system is strained the same way from an additional patient — regardless rich patriarch or poor construction worker — taking up a hospital bed and receiving intensive care on a ventilator. Isolating infections in vulnerable concentrated groups would have gone a long way to helping the entire nation in its COVID-19 battle. We help ourselves by helping others, through alleviating crowded unhealthy accommodations and lifting the vulnerable. For COVID-19 those vulnerable can be rich seniors living in crowded nursing homes; vacationers holidaying on a cruise ship; detainees cramped together in prisons; poor families densely huddled in shanty-towns, slums, decrepit public housing, and favelas; or, in Singapore's case, foreign workers jam-packed in dormitories.

Second, increasing returns in vaccine production mean that profit-seeking pharmaceutical companies hardly ever find it worth their while to engage sufficiently in vaccine-making, with or without their acquiring monopoly intellectual property rights. Producing vaccines entails large fixed costs; intensive testing on human subjects typically takes up to 18 months. While that is happening, company stockholders are wondering why no returns are manifest from all the science and research. As such, in normal business life, vaccine discovery and production are not high-priority items. And although a pandemic means vaccine demand will be widespread and high, the outbreak's sudden vanishing also means profit opportunities can quickly and unexpectedly disappear. Private, profit-driven companies stay away from such markets. Instead, for society to be safe, government stockpiles and public production of vaccine will almost always be needed. The state legitimately provides science and research and development, when externalities mean the private sector will never do so sufficiently.

The Bottom Line

What will the post–COVID-19 world look like? I have focused on just economic life in this article, but even just here there are already clear fault-lines that need repair. I have told a story about a fast car and a sturdy car: we can guide our economy to become the speedy, finely tuned machine that on a clear road comes in first every time; but if it hits a bump, stops dead in its tracks. Or, we can ask that our economy be sturdier, capable of withstanding unexpected knocks; one that does not always top league tables in normal times, but always crosses the finish line.

The critical tradeoff is between driving an economic system to maximal efficiency, on the one hand, and on the other, building in redundancies and resilience through spare back-up capacity. Government intervention is needed to repair the problems created by externalities in health systems.

Post–COVID-19, the new focus will more sharply concentrate on individual well-being and individual responsibility. Old political dogmas about individual rights on the one hand, and state surveillance and control on the other will need to be re-calibrated. In a world of spill overs, individual rights are immediately social. COVID-19 has shown how our economic life is rife with externalities, where we will ourselves rise, only by lifting others around us.

Printed in the United States
by Baker & Taylor Publisher Services